Glencoe

PHYSICAL
SCIENCE

REINFORCEMENT
Teacher Edition

GLENCOE
McGraw-Hill

New York, New York   Columbus, Ohio   Mission Hills, California   Peoria, Illinois

A GLENCOE PROGRAM
Glencoe Physical Science

Student Edition
Teacher Wraparound Edition
Study Guide, SE and TE
Reinforcement, SE and TE
Enrichment, SE and TE
Concept Mapping
Critical Thinking/Problem Solving
Activity Worksheets
Chapter Review
Chapter Review Software
Laboratory Manual, SE and TE
Science Integration Activities

Transparency Packages:
    Teaching Transparencies
    Section Focus Transparencies
    Science Integration Transparencies

The Glencoe Science Professional Development Series
    Performance Assessment in the Science Classroom
    Lab and Safety Skills in the Science Classroom
    Cooperative Learning in the Science Classroom
    Alternate Assessment in the Science Classroom
    Exploring Environmental Issues

Cross-Curricular Integration
Science and Society Integration
Technology Integration
Multicultural Connections
Performance Assessment
Assessment
Spanish Resources
MindJogger Videoquizzes and Teacher Guide
English/Spanish Audiocassettes
CD-ROM Multimedia System
Interactive Videodisc Program
Computer Test Bank—
    DOS and Macintosh Versions

TO THE TEACHER

Reinforcement worksheets in *Glencoe Physical Science* provide an additional method for reviewing the concepts within the numbered sections, or lessons, of each chapter. These exercises are designed to focus on science content and less on vocabulary, although a knowledge of the section vocabulary will be helpful to the student. Reinforcement worksheets are designed for the full range of students in your class, but they will be more challenging for your lower ability students and more of a review for your more able students. Answers appear on reduced pages at the end of the booklet.

Glencoe/McGraw-Hill
A Division of *The McGraw-Hill Companies*

Send all inquiries to:
Glencoe/McGraw-Hill
936 Eastwind Drive
Westerville, OH 43081

Printed in the United States of America

ISBN   0-02-827893-3

2 3 4 5 6 7 8 10 POH 02 01 00 99 98 97 96

TABLE OF CONTENTS

TABLE OF CONTENTS (continued)

• Science Is Everywhere

Use the definitions of pure science and technology listed below to decide whether the discovery described in each statement is an example of pure science or technology. Write a P for pure science or a T for technology in the space provided.

pure science: the study of a subject for the advancement of knowledge
technology: the application of scientific knowledge to improve the quality of life

_____ 1. Sarah observed that the shape of the moon seems to change slightly each night.

_____ 2. A scientist observed that coating glass with certain materials helped to prevent the glass from shattering.

_____ 3. A meteorologist discovered that a radar system developed to track the paths of airplanes could also be used to track the paths of storms.

_____ 4. While on a field trip, a geology student discovers a new kind of mineral.

_____ 5. A biologist discovered that bacteria could not grow in an environment where a certain kind of mold was present. The mold was later used to make the drug penicillin.

Place a check mark beside each item that is likely to be studied by a physical scientist.

_____ 6. the energy given off by the sun

_____ 7. which bones make up the human body

_____ 8. the composition of the bones in the human body

_____ 9. the temperature at which ice melts

_____ 10. the substances that make up a drug

_____ 11. the distance from the sun to Earth

_____ 12. the fish population in a pond

_____ 13. the speed at which electricity travels through a certain kind of wire

_____ 14. how heat from the sun can be used to heat a home on Earth

_____ 15. when the next bird migration occurs

_____ 16. the amount of precipitation that falls in a desert

_____ 17. the chemical makeup of a newly discovered mineral

Chapter 1
REINFORCEMENT

• Finding Out

Complete the following.

1. How does a problem differ from an exercise? _____

_____

_____

Identify the sense you would use to make each of the following observations.

_____ 2. the distance between two points

_____ 3. the loudness of a stereo system

_____ 4. the saltiness of a stew

_____ 5. the number of students in a classroom

_____ 6. determining whether bathwater was too hot or too cold

_____ 7. determining whether milk in a container has soured

_____ 8. the spiciness of a dinner

Identify the sense that each object listed is designed to help.

_____ 9. hearing aid

_____ 10. microscope

_____ 11. thermometer

_____ 12. ruler

_____ 13. stereo headphones

_____ 14. telescope

_____ 15. stethoscope

Place the following terms in logical order by writing the numbers 1 through 4 in the spaces provided.

_____ 16. theory

_____ 17. scientific law

_____ 18. hypothesis

_____ 19. problem

20. What is an experiment? _____

_____

Chapter 1

REINFORCEMENT

• Getting Real
with Special Effects

Write your answers to the following questions and activities in the spaces provided.

1. Why are special effects used in movies? _____

    _____

    _____

2. Compare the composition of special-effects rocks and boulders used in old movies with the

    composition of those used in modern movies. How have new materials improved special-

    effects rocks? _____

    _____

    _____

    _____

    _____

3. Compare the composition of special-effects glass used in old movies with the composition of

    glass used in modern movies. _____

    _____

    _____

4. How have new materials improved special-effects glass? _____

    _____

    _____

    _____

5. Describe the processes of claymation and go-motion. _____

    _____

    _____

    _____

    _____

• Exploring Science

Complete the following.

1. Place the following in logical order by writing the numbers **1** through **5** in the spaces provided.

   _____ **a.** analysis and conclusion   _____ **d.** observations and data

   _____ **b.** hypothesis   _____ **e.** problem

   _____ **c.** procedure

2. Is an experiment an example of an exercise or a problem? Why? _____

   _____

   _____

3. Why is a control important in an experiment? _____

   _____

4. Why is it important to follow all directions in an experiment carefully? _____

   _____

   _____

5. What two articles of clothing should always be worn when working in a science laboratory?

   _____

Match each safety symbol in Column II with its description in Column I. Write the letter of the correct symbol in the blank on the left.

Column I

_____ **6.** fire safety

_____ **7.** electrical safety

_____ **8.** sharp objects

_____ **9.** eye safety

_____ **10.** clothing protection

Column II

a.

b.

c.

d.

e.

• Standards of Measurement

Fill in the missing information in the table below.

SI prefixes and their meanings	
Prefix	**Meaning**
	0.001
	0.01
deci-	0.1
	10
hecto-	100
	1000

Circle the larger unit in each pair of units.

1. millimeter, kilometer

2. decimeter, dekameter

3. hectogram, decigram

4. centimeter, millimeter

5. hectogram, kilogram

6. *In SI, the base unit of length is the meter. Use this information to arrange the following units of measurement in the correct order from smallest to largest. Write the number 1 (smallest) through 7 (largest) in the spaces provided.*

_____ **a.** kilometer

_____ **b.** centimeter

_____ **c.** meter

_____ **d.** dekameter

_____ **e.** hectometer

_____ **f.** millimeter

_____ **g.** decimeter

Use your knowledge of the prefixes used in SI to answer the following questions in the spaces provided.

7. One part of the Olympic games involves an activity called the decathlon. How many events do you think make up the decathlon?_____

8. How many years make up a decade? _____

9. How many years make up a century?_____

10. What part of a second do you think a millisecond is? _____

Chapter 2

REINFORCEMENT

• Using SI Units

1. Complete the table below by supplying the missing information.

Measurement	Base unit	Symbol
	meter	
mass		
	second	
temperature		

In each of the following, circle the units that would most likely be used to express each kind of measurement. You may circle more than one answer for each item.

2. Volume of a solid: mL m³ cm³ L

3. Volume of a liquid: mL mg cm³ L

4. Density of a material: g g/cm³ kg/m³ L

5. Temperature: °K K °C Kg

6. Mass: kg K cm³ mg

7. Time: kg K s mm

8. Length: K km m cm

For each pair of equations, write the letter of the equation that expresses an equal value.

_____ **9. a.** 1 L = 1 dm³   **b.** 1 L = 1 cm³

_____ **10. a.** 1 mL = 1 cm³   **b.** 1 cm³ = 1 L

_____ **11. a.** 0°C = –273 K   **b.** 0 K = –273°C

_____ **12. a.** 1 kg = 100 g   **b.** 1000 g = 1 kg

_____ **13. a.** 400 cm = 4.0 m   **b.** 400 cm = 0.40 m

_____ **14. a.** 1 dm = 10 m   **b.** 1 dm = 0.10 m

_____ **15. a.** 100°C = 373 K   **b.** 373 K = 10°C

16. Calculate the volume of the box in the diagram.

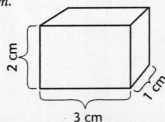

• Graphing

Use the graphs below to answer the following questions.

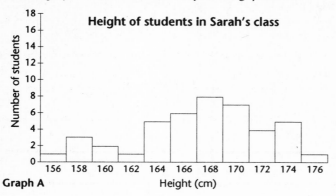

Height of students in Sarah's class

Graph A

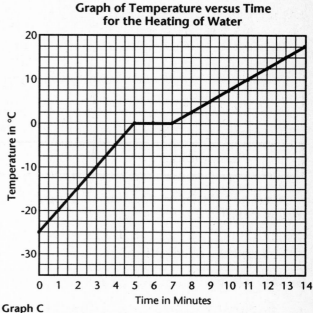

Graph of Temperature versus Time
for the Heating of Water

Graph C

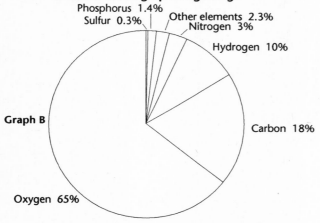

Elements making up living things

Graph B

1. What type of graph is graph A? _____

2. What information is shown on graph A? _____

3. What height do the greatest number of students in Sarah's class have in common? _____

4. What type of graph is graph B? _____

5. What information is shown in graph B? _____

   _____

6. What element makes up the largest part of living things? _____

7. What type of graph is shown in C? _____

8. What does graph C show? _____

9. What is the dependent variable in graph C? _____

10. What is the independent variable in graph C? _____

11. On what axis is the independent variable plotted? _____

12. On what axis is the dependent variable plotted? _____

Chapter 2

REINFORCEMENT

● SI for All?

In the second column of the table below, identify an everyday unit that you would use to measure each item listed. In the last column, identify the SI unit you would use to measure the same quantity.

Item	Everyday unit	SI unit
1. Gasoline		
2. Length of a room		
3. Distance to another town		
4. Milk		
5. Ground beef		
6. Length of a football field		
7. Canned vegetables		

Solve the following problems. Show your calculations in the space below each problem.

8. Sam is 75 inches tall. How tall is Sam in feet?

9. Sam is 190.5 centimeters tall. How tall is Sam in meters?

10. One pound of ground beef costs $2.69. What is the cost of ground beef per ounce?

11. One kilogram of ground beef costs $1.22. What is the cost of the ground beef per gram?

Answer the following question.

12. Is it easier to convert from one unit to another using everyday units or using SI units?

Explain your answer. _____

_____

_____

_____

Chapter 5

REINFORCEMENT

• Temperature and Heat

Determine whether the italicized term makes each sentence true or false. If the statement is true, write the word "true" in the blank. If the statement is false, write in the blank the term that makes the statement true.

_____ **1.** The particles that make up a sample of matter have *kinetic* energy.

_____ **2.** The more *mass* a material has, the greater its temperature.

_____ **3.** As the temperature of a material increases, the particles move more *slowly* and their average kinetic energy becomes greater.

_____ **4.** *Thermal* energy is the total energy of the particles in a material.

_____ **5.** The energy that flows from something with a higher temperature to something with a lower temperature is *thermal energy*.

_____ **6.** Heat is measured in *Celsius degrees*.

_____ **7.** Heat and *work* both involve transfers of energy.

_____ **8.** At 22°C, a football has *less* thermal energy when it is sitting on the ground than when it is moving through the air.

_____ **9.** The kinetic and potential energy of the particles in a material determine its *thermal energy*.

_____ **10.** Different kinds of matter have *different* thermal energies.

_____ **11.** Heat energy flows from *warmer to cooler* materials.

_____ **12.** Mass, kind of matter, and the average kinetic energy of its particles determine the *temperature* of a material.

_____ **13.** Temperature is measured in *degrees*.

_____ **14.** The particles in a cup of cold coffee move more *quickly* than the particles in an equal-sized cup of hot coffee.

_____ **15.** Energy transferred when a force acts over a distance is *heat energy*.

Chapter 5
REINFORCEMENT

Use with Text Pages 138–140

• Thermal Pollution: Waste You Can't See

Determine whether the italicized term makes each statement true or false. If the statement is true, write the word "true" in the space provided. If the statement is false, write in the blank the term that makes the statement true.

_____ 1. Much of the energy used in everyday life ends up as *useful* thermal energy that is given off to the surroundings.

_____ 2. The heat removed from *air-conditioned* buildings and vehicles is released to the outside air.

_____ 3. Thermal pollution occurs when waste heat significantly *cools* the temperature of the environment.

_____ 4. Thermal pollution may be a problem in areas where power plants and factories use *water* to warm their buildings and equipment.

_____ 5. A cooling tower is a device that is designed to cool *air*.

_____ 6. The heat from warmed water dumped into a waterway *lowers* the dissolved oxygen content of the waterway.

_____ 7. The temperature of the water discharged from an electric power plant typically ranges from 5 to 11 Celsius degrees *below* the temperature of the waterway that is receiving the discharge.

_____ 8. A possible use of thermal energy in wastewater is to heat *greenhouses*.

Answer the following questions on the lines provided.

9. What ecological effects might dumping warmed water into a waterway have? _____

_____

_____

_____

10. How does a cooling tower function? _____

_____

Chapter 5
REINFORCEMENT

● Measuring Thermal Energy

Answer the following questions about specific heat and thermal energy on the lines provided.

1. Change in thermal energy can be calculated using the equation $Q = m \times \Delta T \times C_p$.

   a. In this equation, what does Q represent? _____

   b. What does m represent? _____

   c. What does ΔT represent? _____

   d. What does C_p represent?_____

   e. What does the symbol Δ mean? _____

   f. Why is the symbol Δ used with T but not Q?_____

   _____

   g. In what units is T measured?_____

   h. In what units is specific heat measured?_____

   _____

   i. In what unit is m measured? _____

2. What formula is used to calculate ΔT?

   _____

3. Suppose that the temperature of 500 g of water changes from 25°C to 34°C over a period of two hours. How would you calculate the temperature change of the water?

4. Calculate the quantity of heat that must be transferred to 17.0 g of water to raise its temperature from 15°C to 17°C. Water has a specific heat of 4184 J/kg · °C.

Chapter 6

REINFORCEMENT

Use with Text Pages 152–161

• Thermal Energy on the Move

Determine whether the italicized term makes each statement true or false. If the statement is true, write the word "true" in the blank. If the statement is false, write in the blank the term that makes the statement true.

_____ 1. Materials that are poor conductors are *poor* insulators.

_____ 2. The transfer of energy through matter by direct contact of its particles is *convection*.

_____ 3. The transfer of energy in the form of invisible waves is *conduction*.

_____ 4. Solids usually conduct heat *better* than liquids and gases.

_____ 5. The R-value of insulation indicates its *resistance* to heat flow.

_____ 6. Air is a *poor* heat conductor.

_____ 7. Wind and ocean currents are examples of *conduction* currents.

_____ 8. Energy is usually transferred in fluids by *radiation*.

_____ 9. As water is heated, it expands, becomes *less* dense, and rises.

_____ 10. Dark-colored materials absorb *less* radiant energy than light-colored materials.

_____ 11. Only radiant energy that is *reflected* is changed to thermal energy.

_____ 12. The higher the R-value of insulation the *less* resistant it is to heat flow.

Circle the object in each pair that will take in more heat. In the blank, explain why that object will take in more heat.

13. a silver spoon,   _____

    a wooden log   _____

14. a white shirt,   _____

    a red shirt   _____

15. foil in the sun,   _____

    a sidewalk in the sun   _____

16. single-pane window,   _____

    double-pane window   _____

17. R-5 insulation,   _____

    R-35 insulation   _____

Chapter 6

REINFORCEMENT

● Using Heat to Stay Warm

Answer questions 1–10 about the heating system represented in the flowchart.

A. Furnace heats water to boil.

↓

B. Steam provided by boiling water travels through pipes to a radiator.

↓

C. Steam cools inside radiator and condenses to water.

↓

D. Thermal energy of heated radiator heats air in room.

↓

1. Is the system in the flowchart a hot-water system or a steam-heating system?_____

2. How does the furnace get the energy needed to heat the water?_____

3. How is the thermal energy produced by the furnace transferred to the water? _____

_____

4. Why do the pipes carrying the steam to the radiator need to be insulated? _____

_____

5. How is the thermal energy from the steam transferred to the radiator?_____

6. How is the thermal energy of the radiator transferred to the surrounding air? _____

7. What happens to the steam as it gives up thermal energy inside the radiator? _____

_____

8. How is heat from the air surrounding the radiator transferred to the air in the rest of the

room? _____

9. What happens to the water that is formed inside the radiator? _____

_____

10. What is a radiator? _____

_____

_____

Use with Text Pages 166–171

• Using Heat to Do Work

On each piston below, describe the process that occurs during the step of the four-stroke cycle of a diesel engine. Be sure to identify the location of the piston (up or down) in each step.

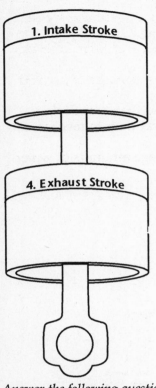

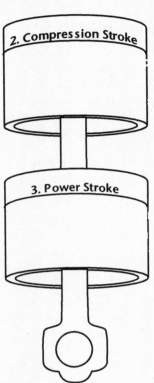

Answer the following questions on the lines provided.

5. How does the four-stroke cycle in a gasoline engine differ from the four-stroke cycle in a

   diesel engine? _____

   _____

   _____

   _____

6. In a car with fuel injection, during which stroke does fuel enter the cylinders? _____

   _____

7. How does the intake stroke of a car with a carburetor differ from the intake stroke of a car

   with fuel injection? _____

   _____

   _____

8. How does an external combustion engine work? _____

   _____

● Energy from the Oceans

Determine whether the italicized term makes each statement true or false. If the statement is true, write the word "true" in the space provided. If the statement is false, write in the blank the term that makes the statement true.

_____ 1. Because the oceans have large surface *currents* and great depths, they can absorb radiant energy from the sun and store it as thermal energy.

_____ 2. Several hydroelectric plants are using the *thermal* energy of tides to rotate turbines and generate electricity.

_____ 3. There can be more than 20°C difference between warm surface water and cold bottom waters in tropical and *subtropical* regions.

_____ 4. Ocean thermal energy conversion (OTEC) is a process that uses *electric* engines to convert differences in ocean water temperature into mechanical energy to drive turbines.

_____ 5. Present OTEC plants have *low* efficiencies because large amounts of water must be pumped from ocean depths.

In the spaces provided, write your answers to the following questions and activities relating to the OTEC heat engine shown in Figure 6-1.

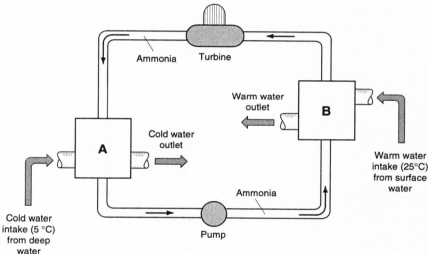

6. Is the ammonia passing through the pump gas or liquid? _____

7. Is the ammonia passing through the turbine gas or liquid? _____

8. What happens to the ammonia in chamber A? _____

9. For the turbine to operate, the ammonia passing through it must have what type of energy?

_____

10. Why must the water passing around chamber A be cold (5°C)? _____

_____

11. What happens to the ammonia in chamber B? _____

12. Why must the water passing around chamber B be warm (25°C)? _____

_____

_____

Chapter 7

REINFORCEMENT

● Why We Use Machines

In the spaces provided, write the equation you would use to calculate each of the following. Use the appropriate symbols in your equations.

1. work _____

2. work input _____

3. work output _____

4. mechanical advantage _____

5. work input and work output in an ideal machine _____

Use the equations you wrote above to solve the following problems. Be sure to use the appropriate units in your answers.

6. A carpenter used a claw hammer to pull a 2-cm nail out of a piece of wood. The nail had a resistance of 1500 N. The carpenter exerted a force of 250 N.

   a. What is the work output of the hammer on the nail?

   b. What was the mechanical advantage of the hammer?

   c. If work input equals work output, what is the work input by the carpenter? _____

Answer the following questions with complete sentences.

7. What are two ways that a machine makes work easier? _____

   _____

8. How does a hammer used to pull a nail from a board change the direction of the force?

   _____

   _____

9. When you use a hammer to drive a nail into a piece of wood, are you changing the size or the

   direction of the force? _____

   _____

   _____

Chapter 7

REINFORCEMENT

• The Simple Machines

Match each simple machine in Column II to its description in Column I. Write the letter of the simple machine in the blank on the left.

Column I

Column II

_____ 1. bar that is free to pivot about a fixed point

a. wheel and axle

_____ 2. an inclined plane with one or two sloping sides

b. inclined plane

_____ 3. grooved wheel with a rope running along the groove

c. gear

_____ 4. two wheels of different sizes that rotate together

d. lever

_____ 5. sloping surface used to raise objects

e. wedge

_____ 6. wheel with teeth along its circumference

f. pulley

_____ 7. inclined plane wrapped in a spiral around a cylindrical post

g. screw

Classify each type of simple machine as either a lever or an inclined plane by writing its name in the proper column of the table.

8. Levers	9. Inclined Planes

Calculate the mechanical advantage for each of the following simple machines.

10. A person uses a crow bar to move a rock that weighs 200 N. The effort arm is 50 cm long. The resistance arm is 20 cm long.

11. A painter uses a fixed pulley to raise a 1-kg can of paint a distance of 10 m.

12. A screwdriver with a 1-cm shaft and a 4-cm handle is used to tighten a screw.

Chapter 7
REINFORCEMENT

• Mending with Machines

Determine whether the italicized term makes each statement true or false. If the statement is true, write the word "true" in the space provided. If the statement is false, write in the blank the term that makes the statement true.

_____ 1. Some parts of your body act as simple machines and are controlled by nerve impulses from your *eyes.*

_____ 2. Organs such as kidneys and hearts can be *transplanted* from one person to another.

_____ 3. *Natural* replacement parts for human bodies are called prostheses.

_____ 4. The science of designing artificial replacements for body parts is called *robotics.*

_____ 5. In the 1700s, Volta observed that *muscles* could be affected by electric shocks.

Use the terms in the box to fill the blanks to the right of the letters below that correspond to the labeled parts of the prosthesis shown in Figure 7-1.

microprocessor	nerve interface	radio transmitter	stump
nerve	prosthesis	receiver	touch sensors

6. a. _____ c. _____ e. _____ g. _____

  b. _____ d. _____ f. _____ h. _____

Answer the following questions with complete sentences.

7. How might the prosthesis shown in Figure 7-15 allow an amputee to feel sensations such as pressure

and texture? _____

_____

_____

_____

_____

_____

8. How might brain-to-computer interfaces help a person regain the use of a dysfunctional limb?

_____

_____

_____

Figure 7-15.

REINFORCEMENT ● **Using Machines**

Use the formula, efficiency = (W_{out} / W_{in}) $\times$ 100%, to calculate the efficiency of each of the following machines.

1. A 600-N box is pushed up a ramp that is 2 m high and 5 m long. The person pushing the box exerts a force of 300 N. What is the efficiency of the ramp?

2. A person uses a fixed pulley to raise a 75-N object 40 m. The force exerted on the object is 120 N. What is the efficiency of the pulley?

Use the formula, power = work/time to calculate the power required in each of the following.

3. A weightlifter lifts a 1250-N barbell 2 m in 3 s. How much power was used to lift the barbell?

4. A crane lifts a 35 000-N steel girder a distance of 25 m in 45 s. How much power did the crane require to lift the girder? Write your answer in kilowatts.

Chapter 8

REINFORCEMENT

● Matter and Temperature

Answer the following questions in the blanks provided. Use complete sentences where appropriate.

1. What are the three common states of matter?

   a. _____   b. _____   c. _____

   What is the fourth state of matter? _____

2. Complete the following chart describing the shape and volume for the three common states of matter.

State of Matter	Volume	Shape

   How does the fourth state of matter differ from the other three?_____

   _____

3. Use the kinetic theory of matter to explain the behavior of the three common states of matter.

   _____

   _____

   _____

   _____

   _____

   _____

   _____

4. In general, when you heat a substance, it expands. This phenomenon is called thermal expansion. Use the kinetic theory to explain thermal expansion. Give an example of thermal

   expansion that you have observed. _____

   _____

   _____

   _____

   _____

Chapter 8

REINFORCEMENT

● Fresh Water: Will There Be Enough?

Write definitions for the following terms in the space provided.

1. fresh water _____

_____

2. polluted water _____

_____

3. thermal pollution _____

_____

Answer the following questions on the lines provided.

4. In what ways can groundwater be polluted by farms? _____

_____

_____

5. What can you do daily in your own life to save water and reduce water pollution?

_____

_____

_____

6. Using Table 8-1 in your textbook, explain why self-service car washes are permitted to stay open when city officials forbid home car washing because of a drought? _____

_____

_____

_____

● Changes in State

Look carefully at the graph. It was drawn from the data collected when a substance was heated at a constant rate. To heat at a constant rate means to add heat evenly as time passes. Use the graph to complete the paragraphs that follow.

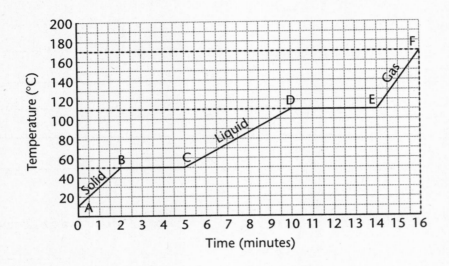

At the start of observations, Point A, the substance exists in the _____ state. The temperature at this point is _____. As energy is _____, the temperature of the substance rises at a constant rate for two minutes. At Point B, the temperature is _____, and the solid begins to _____. The temperature remains constant until the change from solid to _____ is complete. It has taken three minutes to add enough energy to melt the solid completely. From Point C to Point D, the substance is in the _____ state. Its temperature rises at a constant rate to _____. The temperature remains constant while the liquid changes to a _____. At Point E, the substance exists as a _____. Its temperature rises _____ as energy is added.

When the gaseous substance is allowed to cool, it _____ energy. The cooling curve will be the reverse of the warming curve. Energy will be released as the substance changes from a _____ to a _____ and also from a _____ to a _____. The amount of energy released during condensation will be the same as the amount _____ during vaporization.

● Behavior of Gases

Write the definitions for the following terms in the spaces provided.

1. Boyle's law _____

_____

2. Charles's law _____

_____

3. pressure _____

4. absolute zero _____

_____

Explain what will happen in each of the following cases.

5. If the temperature remains constant, what will happen to the pressure of a gas if you

decrease the volume of the container that holds the gas? _____

6. If the volume of a container of gas remains constant, what will happen to the pressure of a

gas if you increase temperature? _____

Answer the following questions regarding temperature.

7. On the Kelvin scale, what is the freezing point of water? _____

8. On the Kelvin scale, what is the boiling point of water? _____

9. On the Celsius scale, what are the freezing and boiling points of water?

_____

• Uses of Fluids

Determine whether the italicized term makes each statement true or false. If the statement is true, write the word "true" in the blank. If the statement is incorrect, write in the blank the term that makes the statement true.

_____ **1.** A fluid is a liquid or a *solid*.

_____ **2.** Buoyancy is the ability of a fluid to exert *a downward* force on an object immersed in it.

_____ **3.** If the buoyant force on an object is *greater than* the weight of the object, the object will sink.

_____ **4.** The buoyant force on an object in a fluid is *equal to* the weight of the fluid displaced by the object.

_____ **5.** *Archimedes'* principle states that pressure applied to a fluid is transmitted unchanged throughout the fluid.

_____ **6.** As the velocity of a fluid increases, the pressure exerted by the fluid *increases*.

_____ **7.** The Venturi effect describes how fluids flow *faster* when forced to flow through narrow spaces.

Answer the following questions on the lines provided.

8. A hydraulic machine can be used to lift extremely heavy objects. Why is the fluid in the hydraulic machine a liquid rather than a gas? _____

_____

_____

9. A block of wood is floating in water. The weight of the part of the block above water is one-third of the total weight of the block. What is the weight of the water displaced by the block of wood? Explain your answer in terms of Archimedes' principle. _____

_____

_____

10. A passenger jet in the air increases its speed. Does the downward force of air on the top of the wings increase or decrease? Does the net lifting force of the air on the wings increase or decrease? Explain your answer. _____

_____

_____

Chapter 9

REINFORCEMENT

● Composition of Matter

Use the words listed below to correctly complete the concept map.

atoms (different)	atoms (same)	colloids	fog
gold	iron	mixtures	muddy water
oxygen	salt	smoke	soft drinks
solutions	substances	suspensions	syrup
vinegar	water	whipped cream	

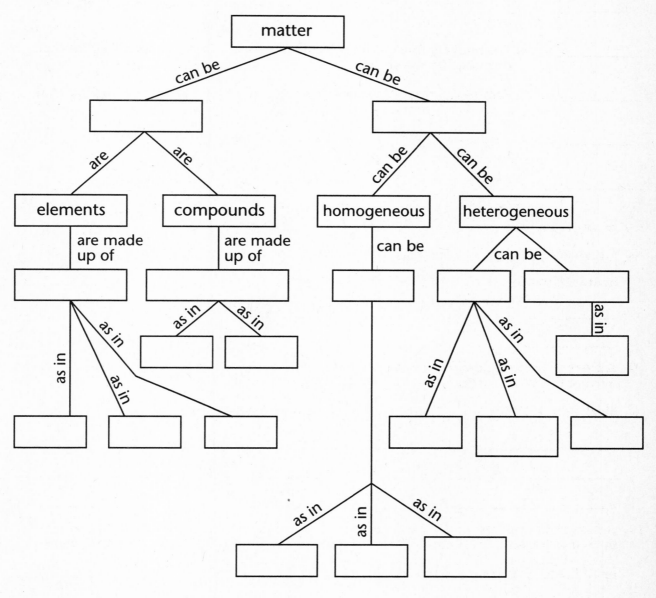

• The Colloid Connection

When Do 50 + 50 = 95?

Read the following paragraphs. Answer the questions and make drawings in the spaces provided.

Karen did an activity in science class. She measured 50 mL of alcohol into one graduated cylinder and 50 mL of water into another graduated cylinder. She then emptied the 50 mL of alcohol into a 100-mL graduated cylinder. Then she emptied the 50 mL of water into the same 100-mL graduated cylinder that contained the alcohol. She then observed and recorded the total volume as 95 mL. Karen thought that she made a mistake in measuring, so she repeated the entire procedure and again observed that the total volume was 95 mL.

How could this be? She asked her teacher what she had done wrong. Her teacher said that Karen would be able to explain the results if she thought about it for a while.

Karen went home from school and made some popcorn. To 500 mL of popped popcorn she added 5 mL of salt and noted that the total volume did not go above 500 mL. Karen then watched her four-year-old neighbor playing in his sandbox. He emptied a container of sand into a pail filled with pebbles, but his pail did not overflow. Karen could not wait until she went to school the next day. She could now explain how 50 + 50 = 95.

1. What explanation was Karen going to give in science class? _____

_____

_____

2. Use these drawings to help you explain.

   a.   b.   c.

3. How can Karen's science class explanation help you explain how air pollution conditions

   can worsen in a city in a period of one day? _____

_____

_____

Chapter 9

REINFORCEMENT

● Describing Matter

Analogies

Below are two sets of words. Complete the second set by choosing a word from those listed below the blank. The two words must be related in the same way as the first set of words.

EXAMPLE
letter:envelope::pillow:[case]
case, sheet, soft, bed

1. steam:water::water: _____
   heat, molecules, ice, matter

2. solid:melting::liquid: _____
   condensing, heating, mixing, vaporizing

3. physical:chemical::size: _____
   burning, taste, solubility, acid

4. liquid:vaporizing::solid: _____
   melting, freezing, decomposing, evaporating

5. iron:rust::silver: _____
   reaction, oxygen, tarnish, water

6. chemical:rust::physical: _____
   compound, condensation, solid, change

7. element:compound::oxygen: _____
   water, hydrogen, matter, mixture

8. compound:mixture::chemical: _____
   physical, separation, property, gas

9. hydrogen:water::carbon: _____
   carbon dioxide, graphite, coal, gas

10. solid:steel::gaseous: _____
    coal, air, water, gasoline

11. burning:candle::corrosion: _____
    vaporization, physical property, copper, mixture.

Chapter 10

REINFORCEMENT

Use with Text Pages 270–275

● Structure of the Atom

Use the clues to complete the puzzle.

Across

3. Scientist who developed the planetary model of the atom
7. Element 105
11. Region surrounding the nucleus which is occupied by electrons
13. Atomic number of fluorine (spelled out)
14. Center of atom
15. Symbol for sodium
16. Symbol for silver
18. Fe is the symbol.
21. Name of element used in fluorescent signs
22. Atom of an element with a different number of neutrons
23. Sum of protons and neutrons
25. Only element with atoms which do not have neutrons

Down

1. Element often made into electrical wire
2. Number of protons in an atom
4. Name of element whose symbol is Ru
5. Negatively charged particle
6. Mixture of mostly nitrogen and oxygen
8. 1/12 the mass of a carbon-12 atom
9. Helps us understand something that we cannot see directly
10. These are like shelves where electrons can be found.
12. Equal in number to the number of protons
14. A particle with approximately the same mass as a proton
17. Element used in balloons
19. Element name of radioactive gas that can accumulate in houses
20. Positively charged particle in nucleus
24. The building block of matter

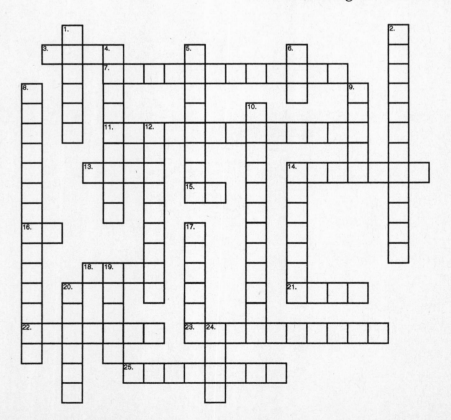

● Smaller Particles of Matter

Answer each of the following questions with one or two sentences.

1. What is a quark? How many types of quarks are known?_____

_____

_____

_____

2. How can scientists study the inner structure of the atom? _____

_____

_____

_____

3. Describe the Tevatron's purpose and how it works. _____

_____

_____

_____

_____

_____

_____

• Masses of Atoms

Isotopes

Answer the following questions on the lines provided.

1. Define isotopes. _____

   _____

   _____

2. How many isotopes can an element have? _____

   _____

   _____

   _____

   _____

3. What is the average atomic mass of an element? _____

   _____

   _____

4. Compare and contrast the atomic structure of the chlorine-35 and chlorine-37 isotopes.

   _____

   _____

   _____

   _____

5. Suppose that a newly discovered element called centium has three isotopes that occur in nature. These are centium-200, centium-203, and centium-209. Assume that these isotopes occur in equal amounts in nature. What will be the average atomic mass of this element?

   _____

   _____

   _____

   _____

Chapter 10

REINFORCEMENT

• The Periodic Table

You will need a scientist's patience to find the names of the 70 elements hidden in the grid. The Lanthanides and the Actinides have been excluded. The same letters may appear in more than one element name. Draw a line through the letters that correctly spell the name of an element.

```
A Y M R                                                              A S S M
R N U E                                                              B L U E
G N T N                                                              E I R G
O O S I                                                              T T O S
N C A D M I U M N                               D E F L U O R I N E H L H U
A I N O E O B O C                               G H P B R O M I N E D A P L
I L O I J E N L H                               K L M U I N E H T U R C S P
M I D N Z E L Y O                               P M Q R T S C M U V H E O H
W S A Y X M D B Z                               Y D U R X E U A S L B L H U
L C R N U R B D D                               P E N I T I F G O H O I P R
E J K I O R L E M                               O E N O D V P R D N L Q T H
K N D G A R T N R                               T H H N I A I S I I A A H E
C N E D S T I U H Y A H E M P E R B E N I T A T S A I A O G N L U U D N I A N
I N I O B I U M O C L E I D E T A N A B E L E G O S C F F E A M L M T T T L I
N U H T N E E L D E U L M B O R O N M L E N N T S S I S L N D L I A G H H L U
M N O B R A C M I S M U I N I T C A L C I U M M U I N O C R I Z L T P A S I M
O R M M M O U T U E I D B U P U T U N E T T V E R U E E O T U U H I E N I U L
E S U L U N G C M N N R M Y M M R O R N T A H T U M S I B I M N M I U U L M N
G M I I I I E E A V U E R M U I R T T Y N T Y I F I R I A I R I D I U M V V E
R U N T S E C M N B M K L I U E M E C H R O M I U M A N L T S U O X Y G E N M
E I A H E L R N I C E M N M D E S E N A G N A M A M P S T R O N T I U M R A N
P L T I N E A D A N B E
P E I U G M I U A R L A
O H T M A U D R M E F D
C M U A M U I M S O L D
```

Reprinted with permission from Games Magazine (2000 Commonwealth Ave., Auburndale, MA 02166) ©1978 by B. & P. Publishing Co. Inc., created by Edith Rudy.

Complete the following paragraphs about the periodic table by filling each blank with the correct term.

In the modern periodic table, elements are listed by increasing _____.

Each box represents an _____. A box contains the name, atomic

number, _____, and _____ for the element.

Vertical columns in the table are called _____. Most elements in a

column have the same number of _____ in the outer energy level and tend to

have similar _____.

Horizontal rows in the table are called _____. The elements on the left side of the

table are _____. Groups 3–12 contain metals known as _____.

Elements on the right side are _____.

REINFORCEMENT • **Why Atoms Combine**

Each statement below contains a pair of terms or phrases in parentheses. Circle the term or phrase that makes each statement true.

1. Most of the matter around you is in the form of (elements, compounds).

2. The properties of a compound are (the same as, different from) the properties of the elements that make up the compound.

3. Na and Cl are (chemical symbols, chemical formulas).

4. NaCl and NaOH are (chemical symbols, chemical formulas).

5. H_2O is the formula for (salt, water).

6. In the formula H_2O, the number 2 is a (subscript, superscript).

7. In the formula HCl, the ratio of hydrogen atoms to chlorine atoms is (1:1, 2:1).

8. The number 2 in the formula H_2O tells you that each unit of this compound contains (2 hydrogen atoms, 2 oxygen atoms).

9. If a symbol in a chemical formula does not have a subscript after it, a unit of that compound contains (0 atoms, 1 atom) of that element.

10. In the formula Fe_2O_3, the ratio of iron atoms to oxygen atoms is (3:2, 2:3).

11. An atom is chemically stable if its outer energy level (is filled with, contains no) electrons.

12. For atoms of most elements, the outer energy is filled when it has (3, 8) electrons.

13. The noble gases do not readily form compounds because they (are, are not) chemically stable.

14. A chemical bond is a (force, chemical) that holds together the atoms in a compound.

15. Chemical bonds form when atoms lose, gain, or (share, multiply) electrons.

Complete the table below by using the formula of each compound to identify the elements that each compound contains and the ratios of those elements. The first one has been done for you as an example.

Formula	Elements in compound	Ratios
H_2O	hydrogen, oxygen	2:1
NaOH		
NaCl		
NH_3		
H_2SO_4		
SiO_2		

Chapter 11

REINFORCEMENT

Use with Text Pages 304–311

● Kinds of Chemical Bonds

Answer the questions about the diagram shown below. Write your answers in the spaces provided.

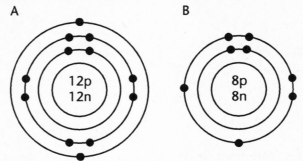

A   B

1. How many electrons will atom A lose to atom B? _____

2. What kind of chemical bond will be formed between atom A and atom B if atom A loses

   electrons and atom B gains these electrons? _____

3. If atom A gives up electrons to atom B, what will the electrical charge of atom A be?

   _____

4. If atom B gains electrons from atom A, what will the electrical charge of atom B be? Why?

   _____

   _____

5. What is an atom with an electrical charge called? _____

6. If atom A and atom B form a compound, what will the total charge of the compound be?

   Why? _____

   _____

Complete the table comparing ionic compounds and covalent compounds.

Characteristic	Ionic	Covalent
How formed		
Smallest particles		
Usual state of compound at room temperature		

Chapter 11
REINFORCEMENT

Use with Text Pages 312–313

• Hazardous Compounds at Home

Classify each of the hazardous materials listed in the table below as toxic, corrosive, or flammable. Place a check mark (✔) in the correct column of the table. More than one column may be checked.

Product	Toxic	Corrosive	Flammable
Insect spray			
Gasoline			
Paint thinner			
Battery acid			
Bleach			
Antifreeze			
Drain cleaner			
Oven cleaner			
Kerosene			
Toilet cleaner			
Disinfectants			

Answer the following questions on the lines provided.

1. How is a corrosive material harmful to the human body?_____

_____

2. How can hazardous materials that get into the groundwater supply be harmful to humans?

_____

_____

3. What kinds of products can be used in place of aerosols? _____

4. How would you share your knowledge of hazardous household chemicals with others?

_____

5. What is a safe alternative to using drain cleaner to unplug a clogged drain?

_____

6. What does *toxic* mean? _____

7. Why should household cleaning products be stored in a place where children and animals

cannot easily get them? _____

_____

8. What should you do with the oil you remove from a car during an oil change?

_____

Chapter 11

REINFORCEMENT

Use with Text Pages 314–320

• Formulas and Names of Compounds

Use the Periodic Table of Elements on pages 286–287 of your textbook to identify the oxidation numbers of the elements in each group.

_____ **1.** any element in Group 1

_____ **2.** any element in Group 17

_____ **3.** any element in Group 2

_____ **4.** any element in Group 18

_____ **5.** any element in Group 16

Answer the following questions in the spaces provided. Use the periodic table if you need help.

1. What is the usual oxidation number of oxygen? _____

2. What is the usual oxidation number of hydrogen? _____

3. What name is given to many of the elements that have more than one oxidation number?

_____

4. What is the sum of the oxidation numbers in a compound? _____

5. What is an oxidation number? _____

_____

_____

Write the formulas for the following compounds. Use the Periodic Table of the Elements in your textbook for help.

1. copper(II) sulfate _____

2. calcium chloride _____

3. iron(II) oxide_____

4. copper(I) oxide_____

5. sodium sulfide _____

Complete the following table by providing the name of the compound and the total number of atoms in each formula given.

Formula	Name	Number of atoms
NH_4OH		
NH_4Cl		
Ag_2O		
K_2SO_4		
$Ca(NO_3)_2$		
Na_2S		

Chapter 12

REINFORCEMENT

• Metals

Complete the table below by writing the name of each of the following metals under the correct heading. Use the periodic table on pages 286–287 of your textbook if you need help.

beryllium	cadmium	calcium	cesium
strontium	cobalt	copper	francium
gold	lithium	magnesium	mercury
potassium	iron	nickel	silver
sodium	zinc	radium	

Alkali metals	Alkaline earth metals	Transition elements	

Write the letter of the term or phrase that best completes each statement.

_____ 1. The elements that make up the iron triad are _____.
   a. radioactive   c. alkali metals
   b. magnetic   d. alkaline earth metals

_____ 2. The alkaline earth metals make up _____ of the periodic table.
   a. group 1   b. group 2   c. group 17   d. group 18

_____ 3. The alkali metals make up _____ of the periodic table.
   a. group 1   b. group 2   c. group 16   d. group 18

_____ 4. The transition elements are in groups _____ .
   a. 1–12   b. 3–13   c. 3–12   d. 3–5

_____ 5. Typical transition elements are metals that have _____ electrons in their outer energy levels.
   a. one   b. one or two   c. three   d. three or four

_____ 6. The most highly reactive of all metals are the _____ .
   a. coinage metals   c. iron triad
   b. alkaline earth metals   d. alkali metals

Chapter 12

REINFORCEMENT

● New Elements, New Properties

Use the periodic table on pages 286–287 of your textbook to answer questions 1–8.

1. What is the name of the group of elements with atomic numbers of 58–71? _____

2. What is the name of the group of elements with atomic numbers 90–103? _____

3. In what period do the elements in the actinide series belong? _____

4. In what period do the elements in the lanthanide series belong? _____

5. How many elements make up the lanthanide series? _____

6. **a.** Which element in the lanthanide series has the highest atomic number? _____

   b. What is the atomic mass of this element? _____

7. **a.** Which element in the actinide series has the greatest atomic number? _____

   b. How many protons are in the nucleus of one atom of this element? _____

8. List the names of the elements that make up the lanthanide series in order from greatest atomic mass to least atomic mass. _____

   _____

   _____

9. How does the lanthanide series compare to the actinide series? _____

   _____

10. What is one practical use of the element americium?_____

    _____

11. Which elements in the actinide series are transuranium elements?_____

    _____

    _____

Chapter 12

REINFORCEMENT

● Nonmetals

Complete the following table that compares the properties of metals and nonmetals by supplying the information requested.

Characteristic	Metal	Nonmetal
Appearance of solid		
Is it malleable?		
Is it ductile?		
Does it conduct heat well?		
Does it conduct electricity well?		
Most common state at room temperature		
Type(s) of bonding		

In the spaces provided, list two properties for each nonmetal listed.

1. Hydrogen _____

2. Fluorine _____

3. Chlorine _____

4. Bromine _____

5. Iodine _____

6. Helium _____

7. Neon _____

Answer the following questions on the lines provided.

8. How does helium differ from the other noble gases? _____

_____

_____

9. How does bromine differ from the other nonmetals? _____

_____

10. How does the location of hydrogen on the periodic table differ from the locations of the other

nonmetals? _____

Chapter 12

REINFORCEMENT

Use with Text Pages 346–351

• Mixed Groups

The elements that make up groups 13–16 of the periodic table are listed below. Classify each element as a metal, non-metal, or metalloid by writing its name under the correct heading in the table. Use the periodic table of the elements on pages 286–287 of your textbook if you need help.

Boron Group	Nitrogen Group	Carbon Group	Oxygen Group
boron	nitrogen	carbon	oxygen
aluminum	phosphorus	silicon	sulfur
gallium	arsenic	germanium	selenium
indium	antimony	tin	tellurium
thallium	bismuth	lead	polonium

Metals	Nonmetals	Metalloids

Allotropes are different forms of the same element having different molecular structures. Diamond and graphite are allotropes of carbon. Look at the diagrams. Label each drawing as the structure for graphite or the structure for diamond.

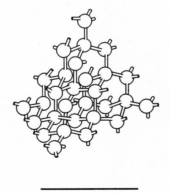

_____

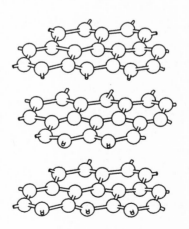

_____

Simple Organic Compounds

Use the structural formulas below to answer the questions.

A.
$$H-\underset{\underset{H}{|}}{\overset{\overset{H}{|}}{C}}-H$$

B.
$$H-\underset{\underset{H}{|}}{\overset{\overset{H}{|}}{C}}-\overset{\overset{H}{|}}{C}=\overset{\overset{H}{|}}{C}-H$$

C.
$$H-\underset{\underset{H}{|}}{\overset{\overset{H}{|}}{C}}-\underset{\underset{H}{|}}{\overset{\overset{H}{|}}{C}}-\underset{\underset{H}{|}}{\overset{\overset{H}{|}}{C}}-\underset{\underset{H}{|}}{\overset{\overset{H}{|}}{C}}-H$$

D.
$$H-\underset{\underset{H}{|}}{\overset{\overset{H}{|}}{C}}-\underset{|}{\overset{\overset{H}{|}}{C}}-\underset{\underset{H}{|}}{\overset{\overset{H}{|}}{C}}-H$$
$$H-\underset{\underset{H}{|}}{\overset{}{C}}-H$$

E.
$$H-\underset{\underset{H}{|}}{\overset{\overset{H}{|}}{C}}-C\equiv C-H$$

1. What is the chemical formula for the compound shown in Figure A? _____

2. What is the chemical formula for Figure C? _____

3. Which compounds are unsaturated hydrocarbons? _____

4. Which compounds are saturated hydrocarbons? _____

5. In Figure B, what is represented by the symbol = ? _____

6. In Figure E, what is represented by the symbol ≡ ? _____

7. What is the chemical formula for Figure D? _____

8. Which two formulas represent isomers of the same compound? _____

9. If the name of the substance in Figure C is butane, what is the name of the substance in

   Figure D? _____

10. What kind of organic compound is shown in all the formulas? _____

• Other Organic Compounds

Identify the following compounds that are aromatic compounds. If the compound is aromatic, place a plus (+) in the space provided. If the compound is not aromatic, place a minus (–) in the space provided.

A.

```
        H
        |
        C
      //   \
  H – C     C – H
      |     ||
  H – C     C – H
      \\   /
        C
        |
        H
```

B.

```
    H
    |
H – C – OH
    |
    H
```

C.

```
    H   O
    |   ||
H – C – C – OH
    |
    H
```

D.

```
    H   H   O
    |   |   ||
H – C – C – C – OH
    |   |
    H   H
```

E.

```
        H
        |
        C
      /   \\
  H – C     C – OH
      ||    |
  H – C     C – H
      \   //
        C
        |
        H
```

F.

```
    OH  OH
    |   |
H – C – C – H
    |   |
    H   H
```

a. _____   c. _____   e. _____

b. _____   d. _____   f. _____

Use the diagrams above to answer the following questions.

1. Which of the compounds is benzene? _____

2. What is the formula for the compound in Figure B? _____

3. Which compounds are substituted hydrocarbons? _____

4. Which of the compounds are organic acids? _____

5. How are the structures of the organic acids similar? _____

_____

6. Which of the substituted hydrocarbons are alcohols? _____

7. What do the alcohols have in common? _____

_____

8. Which compound has the formula $C_2H_4(OH)_2$? _____

9. What symbol is used to show benzene?

10. What is the formula for benzene? _____

• Growing Energy on the Farm

Place a check mark (√) next to each substance that is biomass.

_____ **a.** coal

_____ **b.** wood

_____ **c.** leaves

_____ **d.** gasohol

_____ **e.** animal wastes

_____ **f.** petroleum

_____ **g.** natural gas

_____ **h.** food wastes

_____ **i.** ethanol

Explain how the following terms are related. Write your explanations in complete sentences on the lines provided.

1. methane, natural gas, biogas _____

_____

2. gasohol, biogas, coal _____

3. bacteria, animal wastes, biogas _____

_____

4. energy farming, fuel, biogas _____

_____

5. petroleum, gasohol, ethanol _____

6. biogas, gasohol, environmental problems _____

_____

Chapter 13

REINFORCEMENT

● Biological Compounds

Complete the table below by placing a check mark (√) in the column of each kind of organic compound that has each characteristic.

Characteristic	Protein	Nucleic Acid	Carbohydrate	Lipid
1. enzymes are an example				
2. includes fats and oils				
3. polymers formed from amino acids				
4. is a polymer				
5. always contains carbon and hydrogen				
6. is made up of nucleotides				
7. includes DNA and RNA				
8. RNA controls the production of these				
9. includes sugar				
10. its monomers contain $-NH_2$ and $-COOH$ groups				
11. controls cell reproduction and activities				
12. ratio of hydrogen to oxygen is 2:1				
13. is held together with peptide bonds				
14. glucose is an example				
15. includes starches				
16. includes cholesterol				
17. accounts for 15% of your weight				
18. made up of monomers				
19. molecule is ladder-shaped and twisted				
20. is an organic compound				

Chapter 14

REINFORCEMENT

• Materials with a Past

On the lines provided, write the letters of the substances in Column II that make up each alloy listed in Column I.

Column I

_____ 1. bronze

_____ 2. brass

_____ 3. dental amalgam

_____ 4. aluminum-lithium

_____ 5. steel

Column II

a. copper
b. mercury
c. zinc
d. tin
e. aluminum
f. silver
g. iron
h. carbon
i. lithium

Name one practical use for each alloy listed below.

6. brass _____

7. steel _____

8. bronze _____

9. amalgam _____

10. gold alloys _____

Answer the following questions on the lines provided.

11. What is a ceramic? _____

12. What are structural ceramics? _____

_____

13. What two elements are often mixed with structural ceramics? _____

14. How does glass differ from other ceramics? _____

_____

15. What is the major ingredient in glass? _____

16. What is a cermet? _____

_____

17. List three uses of ceramic products. _____

_____

18. How does adding pigment to glass affect the glass? _____

_____

Chapter 14

REINFORCEMENT

Use with Text Pages 404–405

• Record Breaking with Sports Technology

Complete the following table by listing a new material being used for each type of equipment and one advantage that the equipment has compared with former equipment.

Equipment	New material	Advantage
speed skate blade		
speed skate shoe		
speed skating suit		
skis		
racing car body		
tennis racket		
golf club		

Answer the following questions in complete sentences.

1. Many improvements in sports performance have been brought about by using scientific analysis to change what areas of athletics? _____

   _____

   _____

2. Cite one way in which sports technology might affect sports events and their records.

   _____

   _____

   _____

   _____

   _____

Chapter 14

REINFORCEMENT

• New Materials

Determine whether the italicized term makes each statement true or false. If the statement is true, write the word "true" in the blank. If the statement is false, write in the blank the term that makes the statement true.

_____ 1. A gigantic molecule made from thousands of smaller molecules is called a *monomer*.

_____ 2. Polyethylene is an example of a synthetic *monomer*.

_____ 3. Proteins are examples of natural *polymers*.

_____ 4. Plastics are examples of *natural* polymers.

_____ 5. A material that is made artificially in the laboratory is called a *synthetic* material.

_____ 6. The monomers that make up polyethylene are *nucleic acids*.

_____ 7. A *synthetic fiber* is a strand of a synthetic polymer.

_____ 8. An example of a synthetic fiber is *nylon*.

_____ 9. Most of the raw materials that are used to make plastics come from *protein* products.

_____ 10. Plastic and synthetic fibers are sometimes called *petrochemical* products.

_____ 11. Reinforced concrete is an example of a *plastic*.

_____ 12. Fiberglass is a composite made up of plastic and *concrete*.

Answer the following questions on the lines provided.

13. What does the term *composite* mean?_____

_____

14. What materials are used to make fiberglass?_____

_____

15. How does the use of synthetic products such as plastic increase the use of fossil fuels?

_____

_____

● How Solutions Form

Complete the table below by writing the missing information in the appropriate box. Then answer the following questions.

Solution Type	Solvent	Solute	Example
gas		gas	
		solid	salt water
solid			dental amalgam
	liquid		club soda
	liquid	liquid	
	solid		brass

Study the information in your table carefully. What is true about the state of the solvent and the type of solution produced? _____

_____

Circle the term in parentheses that makes each statement true.

1. A solid dissolves faster in a liquid if the temperature of the liquid is (increased, decreased).

2. A gas dissolves faster in a liquid if the temperature of the liquid is (increased, decreased).

3. The (larger, smaller) the surface area of a solid, the faster it will dissolve.

4. When a gas is being dissolved in a liquid, stirring (speeds up, slows down) the dissolving process.

5. When a solid is being dissolved in a liquid, stirring (speeds up, slows down) the dissolving process.

6. A gas dissolves faster in a liquid when under (high, low) pressure.

Study your responses to the exercise above. Use your responses to answer the following question.

7. How do the methods of speeding the rate of solution for dissolving a solid in a liquid compare to the methods of speeding the rate of solution when dissolving a gas in a liquid?

_____

_____

_____

Chapter 15

REINFORCEMENT

• Regulating Organic Solvents

Write your answers to the following questions and activities in the spaces provided.

1. Why may the buildings in which people live be hazardous to their health? _____

   _____

   _____

2. What are some examples of construction and remodeling materials that contain organic

   solvents? _____

   _____

3. What physical property of organic solvents makes them useful and also makes them

   potentially hazardous? _____

4. In what two ways can organic solvents enter the body? _____

   _____

5. What are some harmful effects of many organic solvents? _____

   _____

   _____

   _____

6. What regulations has the United States Occupational Safety and Health Administration (OSHA)

   established for workers who come into contact with organic solvents? _____

   _____

7. What regulations has the Consumer Product Safety Commission (CPSC) established

   about materials potentially harmful to health? _____

   _____

   _____

8. How does OSHA penalize companies that violate regulations protecting employees?

   _____

   _____

9. Why is good ventilation an important requirement when working with harmful fumes or

   organic solvents? _____

   _____

Chapter 15

REINFORCEMENT

● **Solubility and Concentration**

Use the information in the table to graph the solubility curves for barium hydroxide, Ba(OH)$_2$; copper(II) sulfate, CuSO$_4$; potassium chloride, KCl; and sodium nitrate, NaNO$_3$. Use a different colored pencil for each compound.

Solubility in g/100 g water

Compound	Temperature			
	0°C	20°C	60°C	100°C
Ba(OH)$_2$	1.67	3.89	20.94	101.40
CuSO$_4$	23.10	32.00	61.80	114.00
KCl	28.0	34.2	45.8	56.30
NaNO$_3$	73.0	87.6	122.0	180.00

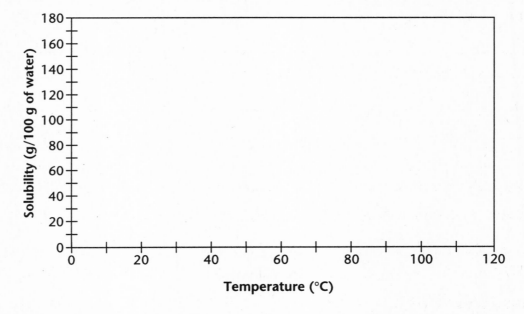

Use the information in the table and your graph to answer the following questions.

1. At about what temperature will 100 g of water dissolve equal amounts of potassium chloride and barium hydroxide? _____

2. At about what temperature will 37 g of both copper(II) sulfate and potassium chloride dissolve in 100 g of water? _____

3. If 100 g of sodium nitrate are dissolved in 100 g of water at 60°C, is the solution formed saturated, unsaturated, or supersaturated? _____

4. If 32 g of copper(II) sulfate are dissolved in 100 g of water at 20°C, is the solution produced saturated, unsaturated, or supersaturated? _____

• Particles in Solution

Use the diagram below to answer questions 1–10.

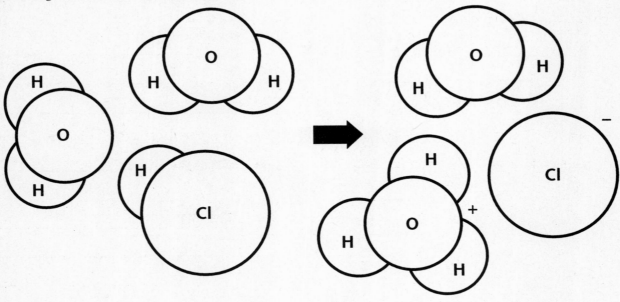

1. Is water a polar molecule or a nonpolar molecule? How do you know? _____

_____

2. Is HCl polar or nonpolar? _____

3. What is the general rule that determines how polar and nonpolar substances dissolve?

_____

4. Will HCl dissolve in water? _____

5. What happens to the HCl molecule when it is placed in water? _____

_____

_____

6. What happens to the hydrogen atom of the HCl molecule? _____

_____

7. What happens to the chlorine atom of the HCl molecule? _____

8. What is the process shown in the diagram called? _____

9. Is HCl an electrolyte or a nonelectrolyte? _____

10. Will the solution conduct electricity? _____

Chapter 16

REINFORCEMENT

• Chemical Changes in Matter

Use the equations to answer the questions.

$$Zn(cr) + S(cr) \rightarrow ZnS(cr)$$

1. What are the reactants in this chemical reaction? _____

2. What is the product? _____

3. What is the state of both the reactants and the products? _____

4. According to the law of conservation of mass, if the total mass of the product in this chemical reaction is 14 grams, what must the combined masses of the reactants be?_____

$$2H_2(g) + O_2(g) \rightarrow 2H_2O(l)$$

5. What is the product in this reaction? _____

6. What are the reactants? _____

7. What are the states of the reactants in this reaction? _____

8. What is the state of the product? _____

9. What do the coefficients tell you about the ratio of the reactants? _____

_____

10. How many units of the product are produced? _____

Write chemical equations for the following reactions.

11. Two units of solid sodium plus one unit of chlorine gas produce two units of sodium chloride, a solid. _____

12. One unit of methane gas, CH_4, plus two units of oxygen gas produce one unit of carbon dioxide gas, CO_2, and two units of liquid water.

_____

13. One unit of aqueous aluminum sulfate plus three units of aqueous barium chloride yield two units of aqueous aluminum chloride plus three units of solid barium sulfate.

_____

Chapter 16

REINFORCEMENT

• Chemical Reactions— Up in the Air

Use the information in Section 16-2 to write the following equations and answer the questions.

1. Write a word equation that explains how chlorine reacts with ozone. _____

   _____

2. Write a chemical equation for the word equation you wrote in number 1. Be sure to indicate

   the state of each substance involved in the reaction. _____

3. What are the reactants in this chemical equation? _____

4. What are the products? _____

5. What allotrope of oxygen has the formula O_3? _____

Answer the following questions with complete sentences in the spaces provided.

6. How do CFCs harm the environment? _____

   _____

7. Why is the ozone layer important to living things? _____

   _____

8. What are CFCs?_____

   _____

9. How are CFCs useful? _____

   _____

10. The number of cases of skin cancer increases as the protection against UV rays from the sun
    provided by the ozone layer decreases. What can you infer about the cause of skin cancer?

    _____

Chapter 16

REINFORCEMENT

● **Chemical Equations**

Answer the following questions with complete sentences.

1. What is a balanced chemical equation? _____

_____

_____

2. Use the law of conservation of mass to explain why a chemical equation must be balanced.

_____

_____

_____

Balance the following equations. If you need help, review the steps for balancing equations on page 449 of your textbook.

3. $H_2(g) + O_2(g) \rightarrow H_2O(l)$

_____

4. $N_2(g) + H_2(g) \rightarrow NH_3(g)$

_____

5. $Li(cr) + FeBr_2(aq) \rightarrow LiBr(aq) + Fe(cr)$

_____

6. $Al(cr) + HCl(aq) \rightarrow AlCl_3(aq) + H_2(g)$

_____

7. $Li(cr) + N_2(g) \rightarrow Li_3N(cr)$

_____

Chapter 16

REINFORCEMENT

• Types of Chemical Reactions

Use with Text Pages 451–455

Match each type of chemical reaction in Column II with its description in Column I. Write the letter of the correct reaction in the space provided.

Column I

_____ 1. A precipitate, water, or a gas forms when two ionic compounds are dissolved in a solution.

_____ 2. Two or more substances combine to form another substance.

_____ 3. One element replaces another in a compound.

_____ 4. A substance breaks down into two or more simpler substances.

Column II

a. synthesis reaction

b. decomposition reaction

c. single displacement reaction

d. double displacement reaction

Classify each of the following chemical reactions as a synthesis reaction, decomposition reaction, single displacement reaction, or double displacement reaction. Write the name of the reaction type on the line on the right.

5. $4Fe(cr) + 3O_2(g) \rightarrow 2Fe_2O_3(cr)$ _____

6. $Zn(cr) + 2HCl(aq) \rightarrow ZnCl_2(aq) + H_2(g)$ _____

7. $MgCO_3(aq) + 2HCl(aq) \rightarrow MgCl_2(aq) + H_2O(l) + CO_2(g)$ _____

8. $NiCl_2(cr) \rightarrow Ni(cr) + Cl_2(g)$ _____

9. $4C(cr) + 6H_2(g) + O_2(g) \rightarrow 2C_2H_6O(cr)$ _____

10. $C_{12}H_{22}O_{11}(cr) \rightarrow 12C(cr) + 11H_2O(g)$ _____

11. $2LiI(aq) + Pb(NO_3)_2(aq) \rightarrow 2LiNO_3(aq) + PbI_2(cr)$ _____

12. $CdCO_3(cr) \rightarrow CdO(cr) + CO_2(g)$ _____

13. $Cl_2(g) + 2KBr(aq) \rightarrow 2KCl(aq) + Br_2(g)$ _____

14. $BaCl_2(aq) + 2KIO_3(aq) \rightarrow Ba(IO_3)_2(cr) + 2KCl(aq)$ _____

Chapter 16

REINFORCEMENT

Energy and Chemical Reactions

Answer the following questions with complete sentences.

1. What is a catalyst? _____

_____

2. What is an exothermic reaction? _____

_____

3. What is an inhibitor? _____

_____

4. What is an endothermic reaction? _____

_____

*Identify whether each reaction described involves a catalyst, an inhibitor, or neither. Write **C** for catalyst, **I** for inhibitor, or **N** for neither in the space at the left.*

_____ **5.** Placing oil on a metal part helps to keep the part from rusting. Is the oil a catalyst, an inhibitor, or neither?

_____ **6.** In the human body, proteins called enzymes help to speed up chemical processes. The proteins are not changed during these chemical processes. Are the enzymes catalysts, inhibitors, or neither?

_____ **7.** Painting a metal surface keeps water from touching the metal and causing the metal to rust. Is the paint a catalyst, an inhibitor, or neither?

_____ **8.** Food preservatives called BHT and BHA slow down the spoilage of certain foods. Are BHT and BHA catalysts, inhibitors, or neither?

_____ **9.** Nickel is used to increase the rate of methane formation from the addition of hydrogen and carbon monoxide. Nickel does not permanently change. Is nickel a catalyst, inhibitor, or neither?

*Identify whether each reaction described below is endothermic or exothermic. In the blank, write **EN** for endothermic or **EX** for exothermic.*

_____ **10.** When a lit match is placed in alcohol, the alcohol ignites producing heat and light.

_____ **11.** Energy in the form of electricity can be added to water to break apart the water molecules into hydrogen gas and oxygen gas.

_____ **12.** A piece of coal placed in a furnace gives off heat and light before turning to ash.

_____ **13.** When ammonium chloride mixes with water, the solution formed feels cold.

• Acids and Bases

Identify each item listed below as to whether it refers to an acid, a base, or both an acid and a base. Use the letters in the key.

KEY: A = acid   **B** = base   **AB** = acid and base

_____ 1. sour taste

_____ 2. bitter taste

_____ 3. produces hydrogen ions in solution

_____ 4. is an electrolyte

_____ 5. is slippery

_____ 6. is often corrosive

_____ 7. exists as a crystalline solid in an undissolved state

_____ 8. produces hydroxide ions in solution

_____ 9. can be detected with an indicator

_____ 10. Soaps are an example.

_____ 11. may be used to make fertilizer

_____ 12. is used in pickling

_____ 13. forms through ionization

_____ 14. forms through dissociation

_____ 15. Compounds that produce this in solution are made up of polar molecules.

_____ 16. produces hydronium ions

_____ 17. Most compounds that produce this in aqueous solution are ionic.

_____ 18. exists in aqueous solution

_____ 19. HCl is an example.

_____ 20. Ammonia is a common example.

_____ 21. conducts electricity

Complete the following. Write your answers on the lines provided.

22. Use the information above to identify four properties that acids and bases have in common.

_____

_____

23. Identify three characteristics of acids that are NOT true of bases. _____

_____

_____

24. Identify three characteristics of bases that acids do NOT have. _____

_____

_____

_____

● Strength of Acids and Bases

The pH values of several common substances are listed below. Place each item from the list on the pH scale in its proper location. The first one has been done for you.

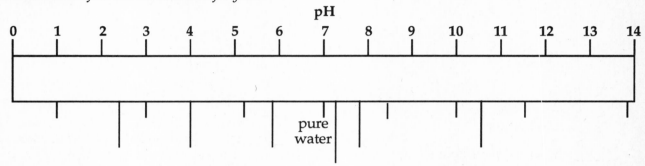

pure water 7.0
ocean water 8.5
tomatoes 4.0
lye 13.8
stomach acid 1.0

lemons 2.5
shampoo 5.8
bananas 5.2
blood 7.2
milk of magnesia 10.5

ammonia 11.5
eggs 7.8
soap 10.0
vinegar 3.0

Complete the table below by writing the name of each of the substances above under the proper heading. Place substances with a pH lower than 3.0 in the strong acids column. Place substances with a pH higher than 10.0 in the strong bases column.

Strong acids	Weak acids	Weak bases	Strong bases

Answer the following questions on the lines provided.

1. Is pure water an acidic, basic, or neutral substance? _____

2. How does the pH of a strong acid compare with the pH of a weak acid? _____

   _____

3. How does the pH of a strong base compare with the pH of a weak base? _____

   _____

4. How does the pH of an acid compare to the pH of a base? _____

   _____

Chapter 17

REINFORCEMENT

• Acid Rain

Determine whether the italicized term makes each statement true or false. If the statement is true, write the word "true" in the blank. If the statement is false, write in the blank the term that makes the statement true.

_____ 1. Normal rain has a pH of *7.0*.

_____ 2. Acid rain is *ten* times more acidic than normal rain.

_____ 3. Any form of precipitation with a pH *higher* than 5.6 is called acid rain.

_____ 4. Scientists think that acid rain forms when *carbonates* of sulfur and nitrogen mix with rainwater.

_____ 5. Sulfur and nitrogen oxides are released when *nuclear fuel* is burned.

_____ 6. Chemical *washers* on smoke stacks can reduce the amount of damaging gases released.

_____ 7. Tiny aquatic *plants and animals* called plankton form the base of the food chain for small fish.

_____ 8. When *plankton* die because of acid rain, the fish that depend upon them for food also die.

_____ 9. Acid rain *melts* important mineral nutrients that are found in soil.

_____ 10. Statues made of limestone and *glass* weather rapidly due to acid rain.

_____ 11. Plants deprived of nutrients because of acid rain do NOT grow at a *normal* rate.

_____ 12. Acid rain causes the most problems in countries that *are not* industrialized.

Chapter 17

REINFORCEMENT

● Acid, Bases, and Salts

Use the equation below to answer questions 1–6.

$$HCl(aq) + NaOH(aq) \rightarrow H_2O(l) + NaCl(cr)$$

1. What type of reaction is shown?_____

2. What are the products in this reaction? _____

3. What are the reactants? _____

4. **a.** Which of the reactants shown is a base? _____

    b. How do you know? _____

5. **a.** Which of the reactants is an acid? _____

    b. What is the name of the acid? _____

    c. Is the acid a strong acid or a weak acid? _____

6. What kind of compound is NaCl? _____

*Identify the type of substance that is most likely to be formed by each reaction described below. Use the terms **soap, salt,** and **ester.***

_____ 7. hydrochloric acid and a base

_____ 8. an organic acid and an alcohol

_____ 9. sodium hydroxide and a fat

_____ 10. acetic acid and methyl alcohol

_____ 11. potassium hydroxide and oil

_____ 12. an acid and ammonia

Answer the following questions on the lines provided.

13. How does a soap made from sodium hydroxide differ from a soap made from potassium

    hydroxide? _____

    _____

14. Why are most laundry products detergents instead of soaps? _____

    _____

15. What is an observable characteristic of an ester? _____

    _____

Chapter 18

REINFORCEMENT

● Characteristics of Waves

On each of the figures below, 1 square of the grid represents 1 unit. Use Figure 1 to answer questions 1–4. On the blank, write the letter of the correct answer.

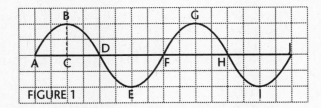

FIGURE 1

_____ **1.** Which distance is exactly 1 wavelength?

    a. A–J   **b.** A–D   **c.** D–F   **d.** B–G   **e.** D–J

_____ **2.** Which distance is the amplitude?

    a. B–C   **b.** A–D   **c.** E–G   **d.** E–I   **e.** A–J

_____ **3.** How many units measure one wavelength?

    a. 2   **b.** 4   **c.** 6   **d.** 8   **e.** 10

_____ **4.** Which letters are the crests?

    a. A, D   **b.** E, I   **c.** H, J   **d.** B, G   **e.** F, H

5. The wave in Figure 2 is identical to the wave in Figure 1. Use a red pencil to draw a wave between points A and B that has a wavelength of 4 units and an amplitude of 2 units.

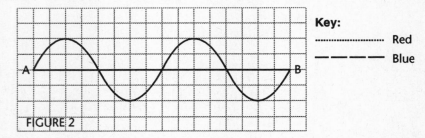

FIGURE 2

Key:
.... Red
— — — — Blue

6. Use a blue pencil to draw a second wave that has a wavelength of 8 units and an amplitude of 4 units.

7. Between points X and Y on Figure 3 draw a wave that has a wavelength of 4 units and an amplitude of 5 units.

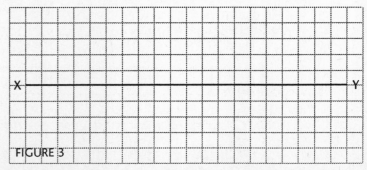

FIGURE 3

Chapter 18

REINFORCEMENT

● The Nature of Sound

Determine whether the italicized term makes each statement true or false. If the statement is true, write the word "true" in the blank. If the statement is false, write in the blank the term that makes the statement true.

_____ **1.** A *rarefaction* is the area of a sound wave where particles are less dense.

_____ **2.** Sound travels more slowly through *gases* than it does through liquids.

_____ **3.** The *amplitude* of a sound is its highness or lowness.

_____ **4.** As the amplitude of a wave decreases, its *intensity* also increases.

_____ **5.** The Doppler effect is an apparent change in the *resonance* of a sound.

_____ **6.** As energy is added to a wave, its amplitude and *intensity* increase.

_____ **7.** The speed of a sound wave depends partly on the *temperature* of the medium.

_____ **8.** The pitch of a sound depends on the *frequency* of the waves that produce it.

_____ **9.** Air and water are examples of *media* through which sound travels.

_____ **10.** A high musical note has a higher *wavelength* than a low note.

_____ **11.** In a *transverse* wave, matter vibrates in the direction the wave travels.

In the drawing below, the freight train and the sports car are traveling beside each other at the same speed and the train whistle is blowing.

12. Compare the frequency of the sound waves produced by the whistle and the pitch of the whistle to each of the following:

a. Michael, who is waiting to cross the tracks at point A _____

_____

b. Sandra, who is driving the sports car _____

c. Tony, who is an engineer on the train _____

d. Jane, whose car has stopped at position B _____

_____

Chapter 18
REINFORCEMENT

• Using Sound Advice in Medicine

Write your answers to the following questions and activities in the spaces provided.

1. What is ultrasonic technology? _____

    _____

2. How do jewelers use ultrasonic sound? _____

    _____

3. How do chemists use ultrasonic technology? _____

    _____

4. What is probably the best-known use of ultrasound in medicine? _____

    _____

5. Physicians commonly use ultrasound to examine what abdominal organs? _____

    _____

6. How is the ultrasound Doppler shift used in medicine? _____

    _____

7. What are kidney stones? _____

8. How has ultrasound replaced surgery as a means of removing some kidney stones?

    _____

    _____

    _____

Sequence from 1–5 the following steps in producing a sonogram, by writing the correct number of the step in the blank to the left of each statement.

_____ Computer program converts electrical signals into video images.

_____ Probe sends out high-frequency sound waves.

_____ Sound waves produce electrical signals.

_____ Sound waves reflect from organs and tissues.

_____ Sound waves strike organs and tissues.

Chapter 18

REINFORCEMENT

• Music to Your Ears

Combine the word parts below to form the answers to the clues below. Work carefully. A space has been left between each word part to help you. Place one letter on each blank, and be sure the number of letters in each word part matches the number of blanks. Cross out each word part as you use it. The first definition has been started for you to use as an example.

a	con	fer	mu	qua	struc	tive	ver
a	cous	fun	noise	re	tal	tive	ver
ance	da	~~in~~	o	res	tave	tion	
beats	de	li	oc	sic	~~ter~~	tones	
ber	ence	men	on	struc	tics	ty	

1. the ability of two or more waves to combine

   I N   T E R   ___ ___ ___   ___ ___ ___ ___

2. effect produced when a musical instrument vibrates

   ___ ___ ___   ___ ___   ___ ___ ___ ___

3. variations of sound intensity

   ___ ___ ___ ___ ___ ___

4. type of interference that results in two waves canceling each other

   ___ ___   ___ ___ ___ ___ ___   ___ ___ ___ ___

5. sound that has no set pattern or definite pitch

   ___ ___ ___ ___ ___ ___

6. describes the difference between two sounds having the same pitch

   ___ ___ ___   ___ ___   ___ ___

7. the study of sound

   ___   ___ ___ ___ ___   ___ ___ ___ ___

8. tone produced when an entire string vibrates up and down

   ___ ___ ___   ___ ___   ___ ___ ___   ___ ___ ___

9. sounds with specific pitches and qualities that follow a regular pattern

   ___ ___   ___ ___ ___

10. frequency range of the musical scale

    ___ ___   ___ ___ ___ ___

11. the type of interference that occurs when two wave crests arrive together

    ___ ___ ___   ___ ___ ___ ___ ___   ___ ___ ___ ___

12. produced by vibrations that are multiples of the fundamental frequency

    ___   ___ ___ ___   ___ ___ ___ ___ ___

13. the effect produced by many reflections of sounds

    ___ ___   ___ ___ ___   ___ ___ ___   ___   ___ ___ ___ ___

● Electromagnetic Radiation

Use the diagram to answer questions 1–9.

Optical

Radio waves	Microwaves	Infrared		Ultraviolet	X rays	Gamma rays
	Long/Short					

→ Increasing frequency →

_____ 1. The wavelength of an electromagnetic wave is _____ .
  a. directly proportional to its frequency   **c.** inversely proportional to its frequency
  b. inversely proportional to its velocity   **d.** none of the above

_____ 2. In a vacuum, all electromagnetic waves have _____ .
  a. the same frequency   **c.** the same wavelength
  b. the same velocity   **d.** all of the above

_____ 3. All electromagnetic radiation in the optical portion of the electromagnetic spectrum
  _____ .
  a. is visible   **c.** has the same frequency
  b. has the same wavelength   **d.** all the above

_____ 4. Compared to the photons of violet light, the photons of red light _____ .
  a. have more energy   **c.** have equal energy
  b. have less energy   **d.** none of the above

_____ 5. Compared to radio waves, microwaves have _____ .
  a. shorter wavelengths   **c.** higher frequencies
  b. photons with more energy   **d.** all of the above

_____ 6. Compared to gamma rays, X rays have _____ .
  a. longer wavelengths   **c.** photons with more energy
  b. higher frequencies   **d.** all of the above

_____ 7. We perceive infrared waves as _____ .
  a. coldness   **c.** warmth
  b. light   **d.** none of the above

_____ 8 Compared to gamma rays, radio waves have _____ .
  a. shorter wavelengths   **c.** photons with less energy
  b. higher frequencies   **d.** none of the above

_____ 9. All objects emit _____ .
  a. gamma rays   **c.** electromagnetic waves
  b. light   **d.** none of the above

Chapter 19

REINFORCEMENT

Use with Text Pages 536–543

● Light and Color

Solve the following crossword puzzle by using the clues provided.

Across

3. Soak up, for example, light rays
5. Colored material that absorbs some colors but reflects others
7. Color that results from mixing red and yellow pigments
8. Primary light colors are this type.
9. Primary pigments are this type.
13. Allows some light to pass without your being able to see through clearly
14. Type of nerve cells on retina that allow you to see dim light
17. Transparent object that allows one or more colors through but absorbs others
18. What an object does to light so we see it

Down

1. Light produced by mixing all colors of the visible spectrum
2. Colors that can be mixed to produce any other colors
4. Color of an object that absorbs all light
6. Nerve cells you use to distinguish colors
10. This type of radiation lies just outside the high-frequency end of the visible spectrum.
11. Allowing nearly all light to pass through
12. What you see when reflected wavelengths of light reach your eyes
15. Material you cannot see through
16. The color you see if you are looking at light that has no red or blue

REINFORCEMENT

• Battle of the Bulbs

1. Write a paragraph about lighting. Use the words listed below in your paragraph.

light bulb	tungsten	phosphorus	light
incandescent light	heat	coating	efficiency
fluorescent light	filament	ultraviolet radiation	

_____

_____

_____

_____

_____

_____

_____

_____

2. Observe incandescent and fluorescent lights in your home, in your school, and in a store or office.

a. Where is each type of light more likely to be used? _____

_____

_____

b. Compare and contrast the color and general appearance of fluorescent and incandescent

lights. _____

_____

_____

c. Why do you think the types of lights were chosen for use in the places that you observed?

_____

_____

_____

_____

• Wave Properties of Light

Fill in the blanks in this diagram of a light wave hitting a smooth, shiny surface.

FIGURE 1

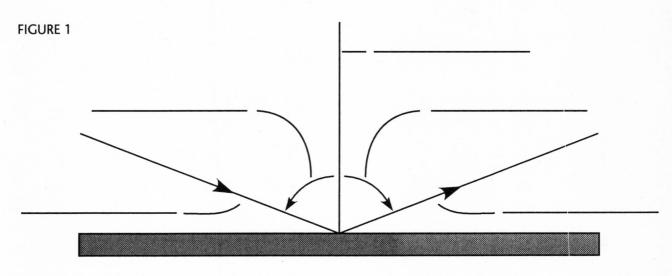

Figure 2 is a sketch of Tanya's fish tank as she looks at it from one of the corners. It appears to Tanya that there are two fish in the tank. However, she knows she has only one fish. Explain why two fish are seen and draw a ray diagram to show what happens. (Hint: The aquarium glass refracts light rays.)

FIGURE 2

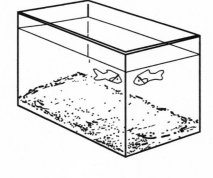

_____

_____

On the blank, write the letter of the term that best completes each of the following statements.

_____ **1.** The interference of light shows the _____ behavior of light.
    a. particle   **b.** translucent   **c.** wave   **d.** refraction

_____ **2.** The bending of light around corners is called _____ .
    a. refraction   **b.** diffraction   **c.** interference   **d.** reflection

_____ **3.** A(n) _____ is used to separate the colors of white light.
    a. diffraction grating   **c.** photon
    b. electromagnetic spectrum   **d.** modulation

Chapter 20

REINFORCEMENT

• The Optics of Mirrors

1. Locate the image of an object placed between the focal point and the center of a concave mirror by drawing two rays. Draw the image and describe this image with words.

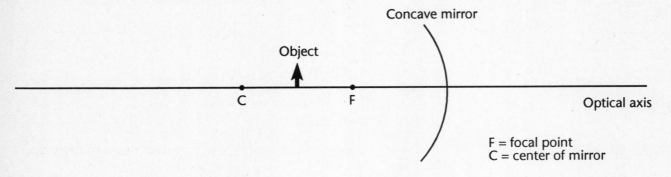

2. Locate the image of an object placed beyond the center of a concave mirror by drawing two rays. Draw the image and describe this image with words.

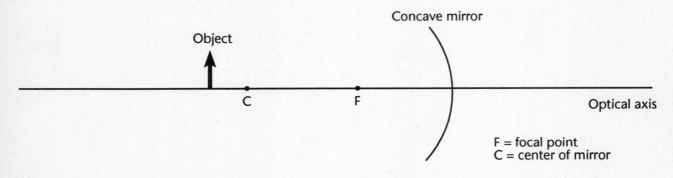

3. What type of mirror would you use to allow a large area to be viewed? _____
   Use rays to show how a virtual image is formed by a convex mirror.

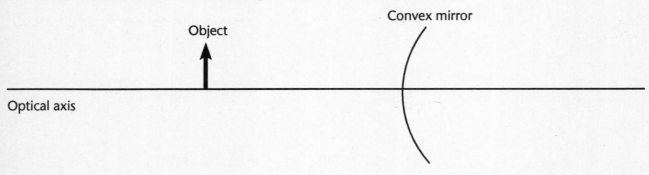

Why do you often see the phrase "Objects are closer than they appear!" written on convex mirrors?

_____

_____

● The Optics of Lenses

In the blank at the left, write the term that correctly completes each statement.

_____ **1.** A type of lens used to correct nearsighted vision is a(n) _____ lens.

_____ **2.** All lenses have a special property. This property is the ability to _____ light.

_____ **3.** A magnifying glass is an example of a(n) _____ lens.

_____ **4.** With normal vision, the image of an object should focus on the part of the eye called the _____ .

_____ **5.** The problem of blurry vision from _____ results from an uneven surface of the cornea.

6. Nearsighted vision is the result of the images of objects being focused in front of the retina.

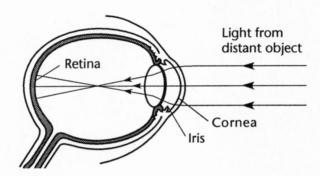

Draw the type of lens in front of the eye below that would be used to correct nearsighted vision. Draw a ray diagram to show how this type of lens corrects nearsighted vision.

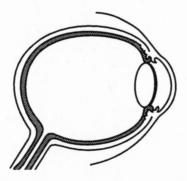

Chapter 20

REINFORCEMENT

• Optical Instruments

1. You are going to assemble a refracting telescope, a reflecting telescope, and a microscope. Which lenses or mirrors will you put in each instrument? Write your answer in the table, using the lenses or mirrors from the list below. Each can be used more than once if needed.

concave mirror
convex lens
plane mirror

Refracting telescope	Reflecting telescope	Microscope

2. Label the parts of this camera using the following terms: aperture, film, lens, and shutter.

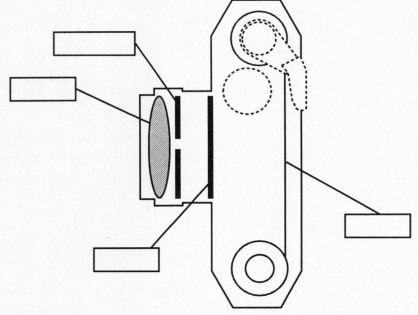

Complete the following paragraph.

Cameras use one or more lenses to focus light on photographic _____.

To focus the light, refraction by the lens creates a _____ image. The light

reaches the film only when the _____ is open. The shutter must be kept

open longer when the light is _____. Another control of the amount of

light to reach the film is the _____ setting. Cameras can have removable

lenses so that lenses of different _____ lengths can be used.

Chapter 20
REINFORCEMENT

Use with Text Pages 572–573

● The Hubble Space Telescope

Write a paragraph describing the Hubble Space Telescope. Use the following terms in your paragraph.

distortion	Hubble	primary mirror
images	galaxies	secondary mirror
orbit	universe	computer software
infrared	expanding	investigation
ultraviolet	solar panels	

_____

_____

_____

_____

_____

_____

_____

_____

_____

_____

Describe the problems and setbacks faced in launching the Hubble Space Telescope into orbit. Use the following terms in your description.

late   software   redesign   delay   testing

_____

_____

_____

_____

_____

_____

_____

_____

Chapter 20

REINFORCEMENT

● **Applications of Light**

Use two or three sentences to respond to the following questions.

1. Why are sunglasses with polarized lenses often worn by people driving long distances?

_____

_____

_____

_____

2. What is laser light? _____

_____

3. Laser light has many practical uses. Briefly describe its use in the following areas.

   a. retail stores and grocery stores _____

   _____

   b. home entertainment systems _____

   _____

   c. medicine _____

   _____

   _____

   d. industry _____

   _____

   e. surveying _____

   _____

   f. astronomy _____

   _____

   g. communications _____

   _____

4. What are optical fibers? What are some of their major uses? _____

   _____

   _____

   _____

Chapter 20

REINFORCEMENT

● Electric Charge

Determine whether the italicized term makes each statement true or false. If the statement is true, write the word "true" in the blank. If the statement is false, write in the blank the term that makes the statement true.

_____ 1. The positively charged particles in an atom are *protons*.

_____ 2. The negatively charged particles of an atom are *neutrons*.

_____ 3. If an atom has an equal number of protons and electrons, the entire atom is electrically *neutral*.

_____ 4. If an atom has a greater number of electrons than protons, the entire atom has a *positive* charge.

_____ 5. The accumulation of electric charges on an object is called *magnetism*.

_____ 6. The electric field caused by an electron is *weakest* near the electron.

_____ 7. An electric field becomes weaker as distance from the electron *increases*.

_____ 8. A conductor is a material that allows electrons to flow through it *easily*.

_____ 9. Metals are *poor* conductors of electricity.

_____ 10. Plastics, rubber, wood, and glass are good *conductors*.

_____ 11. Earth serves as a *conductor* of electricity.

_____ 12. The presence of electric charges can be detected with an *electroscope*.

_____ 13. The leaves of an electroscope hang straight down when the device receives a *charge*.

_____ 14. If both leaves of an electroscope receive a negative charge, the leaves will *attract* each other.

_____ 15. When an object loses electrons, it gains a *negative* charge.

• To Burn or Not

Put the following illustrations showing the formation of lightning in the proper order by writing the numbers 1 (first) through 3 (last) in the spaces provided.

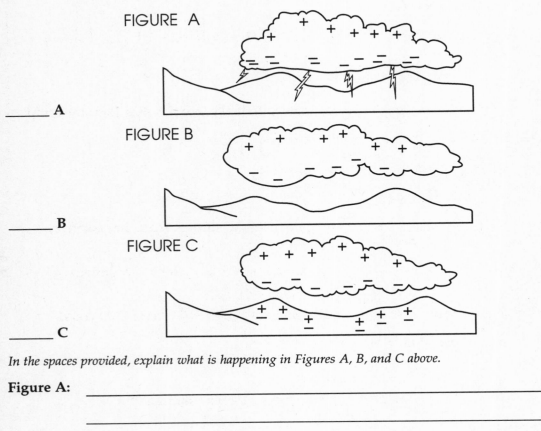

FIGURE A

_____ A

FIGURE B

_____ B

FIGURE C

_____ C

In the spaces provided, explain what is happening in Figures A, B, and C above.

Figure A: _____

_____

_____

Figure B: _____

_____

Figure C: _____

_____

Answer the following questions on the lines provided.

1. How can lightning-induced forest fires be helpful to the environment? _____

_____

_____

2. Why do many buildings have lightning rods? _____

_____

Chapter 21

REINFORCEMENT

• Electric Current

Circle the term in parentheses that makes each statement true.

1. A negatively charged object has electrons with (more, less) potential energy to move and do work than an object that is neutral.

2. Electrons flow from areas of (higher, lower) potential energy to areas of (higher, lower) potential energy.

3. Potential difference is measured in (amperes, volts).

4. Electrons passing through a lamp (gain, lose) some potential energy as they light the lamp.

5. Electrical potential (varies, is the same) in all parts of a circuit.

6. The current in a circuit is measured in (volts, amperes).

7. Current is measured with (an ammeter, a voltmeter).

8. When a dry cell is connected in a series, the flow of electrons moves from the (positive, negative) terminal to the (positive, negative) terminal.

9. In a dry cell, the carbon rod releases electrons and becomes the (positive, negative) terminal.

10. The potential difference between the two holes in a wall socket is (12 volts, 120 volts).

11. A car battery is an example of a (dry, wet) cell.

12. Resistance is measured in (ohms, volts).

13. Copper has a (higher, lower) resistance to electron flow than aluminum.

14. According to Ohm's law, ($I = V/R$, $V = I/R$).

15. The symbol for ohm is (Ω, π).

16. In the equation $I = V/R$, I is expressed in (ohms, amperes).

17. In the equation $I = V/R$, V is expressed in (volts, ohms).

18. The (+, –) terminal of a dry cell identifies the location of the carbon rod.

19. A wire with a resistance of 3Ω has a (greater, lesser) resistance to electron flow than a wire with a resistance of 5Ω.

20. A coulomb is the charge carried by 6.24 (billion, billion billion) electrons.

Use with Text Pages 608–613

• **Electrical Circuits**

Use the diagrams to answer the following questions.

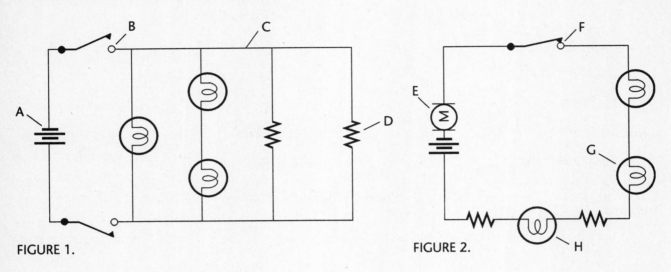

FIGURE 1.   FIGURE 2.

1. What are the diagrams called? _____

2. What kind of circuit is shown in Figure 1?_____

3. What kind of circuit is shown in Figure 2?_____

4. What devices are providing electrical energy in Figure 1? _____

5. What device is shown at B in Figure 1? _____

6. Can current flow through the device shown at B in Figure 1? _____

    _____

7. What is shown at C in Figure 1?_____

8. What does the symbol labeled D in Figure 1 represent? _____

9. What is shown at E in Figure 2?_____

10. What is shown at F in Figure 2? _____

11. Can a current travel through the device shown at F in Figure 2?_____

12. What is shown at G in Figure 2? _____

13. How many paths can electrons follow in Figure 2? _____

14. If the device at G in Figure 2 stops working, what effect will this have on device H? Why?

    _____

    _____

Chapter 21

REINFORCEMENT

Use with Text Pages 614–621

• Electrical Power and Energy

Match each unit in Column II with what it measures in Column I. Write the letter of the correct unit in the blank on the left.

Column I

_____ 1. potential difference

_____ 2. current

_____ 3. electric power

_____ 4. electrical energy

_____ 5. resistance

Column II

a. W or kW

b. Ω

c. V

d. kWh

e. A

Use the equation $P = I \times V$ to find the missing value in each problem. Be sure to use the correct units in your answers.

6. A radio operates with a potential difference of 9 volts. The radio uses 0.9 watt of power. How much current does the radio use?

7. A blow dryer uses 1200 watts of power. Current flow through the blow dryer is 10 amperes. At what potential difference does the blow dryer operate?

8. A lamp operates with a potential difference of 120 volts and a current of 0.25 ampere. How much power does the lamp use?

9. A lamp uses 60 watts of power. It operates with a potential difference of 120 volts. How much current is required by the lamp?

Use the electric meter readings in the table to answer the following questions.

Month	Reading (kWh)
June	6921
July	7923
August	9484

10. How many kilowatt-hours of electricity were used in the 1-month period between June and July?

11. How many kilowatt-hours of electricity were used in the 1-month period between July and August?

12. If electricity costs $0.16 per kilowatt-hour, how much would the electric bills be for the periods June–July and July–August?

● Characteristics of Magnets

Complete the diagrams below as instructed or answer the questions.

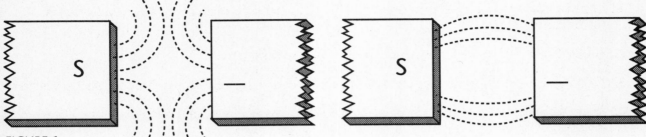

FIGURE 1.

1. The lines in Figure 1 show magnetic forces acting between two pairs of bar magnets. Correctly label the unlabeled poles of the magnets. Write **N** for north and **S** for south on the proper part of each magnet.

2. What generalization can you make about the reaction between like poles?

_____

3. What generalization can you make about the reaction between unlike poles?

_____

4. On Figure 2, draw the lines of force around the bar magnet as they would appear if you sprinkled iron filings around the magnet.

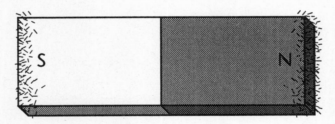

FIGURE 2.

5. Where are most of the iron filings located?_____

6. Where are the iron filings most spread out? _____

7. What can you infer about the strength of a magnetic field based upon the position of the iron

    filings? _____

_____

8. What three materials can be used to make a magnet such as the ones shown above?

_____

Chapter 22

REINFORCEMENT

● Uses of Magnetic Fields

Circle the term in parentheses that makes each statement true.

1. When a current is passed through a coil of wire, (an electromagnet, a commutator) is formed.

2. An electromagnet is a (permanent, temporary) magnet.

3. Adding more turns to the wire coil (increases, decreases) the strength of an electromagnet.

4. Increasing the amount of current that flows through a wire (increases, decreases) the strength of an electromagnet.

5. Electromagnets change electrical energy into (chemical, mechanical) energy.

6. An instrument that is used to detect current is (an electromagnet, a galvanometer).

7. Ammeters are used to measure the (potential difference, electrical current) passing through a circuit.

8. The potential difference of a circuit is measured in (amperes, volts).

9. The potential difference of a circuit is measured with (a voltmeter, an ammeter).

10. An ammeter should be connected (in series, in parallel) with a circuit.

11. A reversing switch in a motor that rotates with an electromagnet is called a (voltmeter, commutator).

12. Billions of nuclei in your body respond to an applied magnetic field when you have (an X ray, an MRI).

The table below compares and contrasts the characteristics of ammeters and voltmeters. Complete the table by filling in the information requested.

Characteristic	Ammeter	Voltmeter
What it measures		
How it's connected		
Units of measurement		

Chapter 22

REINFORCEMENT

• Producing Electric Current

Study the diagram below. In the spaces provided, label each drawing as either a motor or a generator. Label parts a–h as either coil, brushes, commutator, permanent magnet, or shaft.

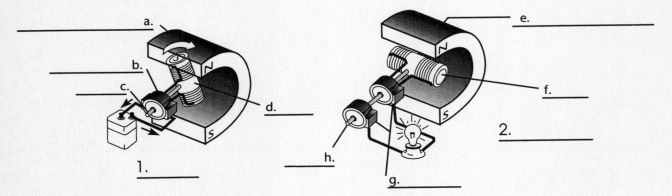

Circle the term in parentheses that makes each statement true.

1. When the wire loop of a (motor, generator) turns, an electric current is produced.

2. The current produced by a generator is (direct, alternating) current.

3. A motor (uses, creates) an electric current as it turns.

4. A device that increases or decreases voltage of a power line is a (transformer, motor).

5. If the secondary coil of a transformer has more turns than the primary coil, the transformer is a (step-up, step-down) transformer.

In the space below, draw a sketch of a step-down transformer that has half as many coils in the secondary coil as it has in its primary coil.

• Superconductivity

Determine whether the italicized term makes each statement true or false. If the statement is true, write the word "true" in the blank. If the statement is false, write in the blank the term that makes the statement true.

_____ 1. As the temperature of a material increases, its resistance *decreases*.

_____ 2. Materials that have no electrical resistance are called *superconductors*.

_____ 3. Absolute zero is *zero degrees Celsius*.

_____ 4. The temperature at which a material becomes a superconductor is called its *resistance* temperature.

_____ 5. Because superconductors have no resistance, a current can flow through them *indefinitely* without losing energy.

_____ 6. Ten percent of the electrical energy that flows through power lines is lost as *light*.

_____ 7. It is hard to shape superconducting materials into wire because they are *flexible*.

_____ 8. Levitating trains do not give off *pollutants*.

_____ 9. A material that allows electrons to flow through it easily is a *conductor*.

_____ 10. One way to cool a material to its superconducting temperature is to immerse it in liquid *copper*.

_____ 11. New materials have been developed that are superconducting at temperatures as high as *120 K*.

_____ 12. Resistance in a material causes energy to be lost as *heat*.

Chapter 23

Use with Text Pages 648–653

REINFORCEMENT

• Semiconductor Devices

Determine whether the italicized term makes each statement true or false. If the statement is true, write the word "true" in the blank. If the statement is false, write in the blank the term that makes the statement true.

_____ 1. Materials that are less conductive than metals but more conductive than nonmetal insulators are *magnets*.

_____ 2. Some *metalloids* are semiconductors.

_____ 3. The conductivity of semiconductors can be *increased* by adding impurities to semiconductor crystals.

_____ 4. The ability of *transistors* to amplify signals makes it possible to use tape recorders and television.

_____ 5. In the periodic table, all the elements located between the metals and nonmetals are *semiconductors*.

_____ 6. A device that can change alternating current to direct current is a *transistor*.

_____ 7. A diode allows *current* to flow in only one direction.

_____ 8. Today's radios can be extremely small because they have *magnetic electrical tape* instead of vacuum tubes.

_____ 9. A semiconductor that increases the strength of an electrical signal is a *rectifier*.

_____ 10. The process by which the strength of an electric current is increased is called *transition*.

_____ 11. An integrated circuit contains resistors, transistors, and diodes on a thin slice of *silicon*.

_____ 12. Electronic equipment that uses integrated circuits requires *more* space than equipment that uses vacuum tubes.

_____ 13. Doping silicon with arsenic *decreases* its conductivity.

_____ 14. The adapter for a radio is a type of *integrated circuit*.

Chapter 23

REINFORCEMENT

● Radio and Television

Use the diagram below to answer questions 1–5.

Wave A

Wave B

1. Is wave A a transverse wave or a compressional wave? _____

2. What kind of wave is wave B? _____

3. Which wave is a radio wave? _____

4. Which wave is a sound wave? _____

5. How does a radio work? _____

   _____

   _____

   _____

Answer the following questions on the lines provided.

6. What does the abbreviation AM stand for? _____

7. What is represented by the abbreviation FM? _____

8. What part of a radio or television set collects radio signals? _____

9. On what part of a television set is the picture produced? _____

10. How does a CRT work? _____

   _____

   _____

Chapter 23

REINFORCEMENT

Use with Text Pages 658–665

• Microcomputers

Place a plus sign (+) beside each statement that agrees with what was said in your textbook. Place a minus sign (–) beside each statement that does not agree. In the space provided, explain why the statement does not agree.

_____ 1. A microprocessor serves as the brain of a computer. _____

_____ 2. The video screen of most computers is a cathode-ray tube. _____

_____ 3. A video screen is an input device. _____

_____ 4. The major permanent components of a microcomputer are referred to as computer

hardware. _____

_____ 5. All information in a computer is processed using the numbers one and two.

_____

_____ 6. The CPU of a computer is contained in the microprocessor. _____

_____ 7. The temporary memory of a computer is called ROM. _____

_____ 8. Because information in RAM is stored electronically, it is lost when the computer is

shut off. _____

_____ 9. Disk drives store information magnetically. _____

_____ 10. Hard disk drives can be removed from the computer for easy storage.

_____

_____ 11. A floppy disk can be used to transfer data from one computer to another compatible

computer. _____

_____ 12. BASIC, Pascal, and Fortran are computer languages used by programmers. _____

_____ 13. A microprocessor is an integrated circuit on the main circuit board of a computer.

_____

_____ 14. Computer memory is expressed in units of CPU. _____

_____ 15. The programs of a computer are often referred to as software. _____

In the spaces provided, identify the term represented by each abbreviation. Then write a definition for each term.

16. RAM   Term: _____

Definition: _____

17. ROM   Term: _____

Definition: _____

Chapter 23

REINFORCEMENT

● Computer Crimes

Decide whether each action described below is a computer crime. Write "Y" in the blank if it is a computer crime. Write "N" in the blank if it is not a computer crime.

_____ 1. You make a backup copy of software you purchased to use if the original becomes damaged.

_____ 2. You make a copy of software you bought to give to a friend.

_____ 3. A friend of yours gives you a copy of the software needed to play a computer game.

_____ 4. You discover that a disk you borrowed from a friend has placed a virus in your computer.

_____ 5. You decide to play a practical joke by placing a computer virus into someone's computer system.

_____ 6. You can access the library computer from your computer. When you input the information needed to get into the subject files, you discover that you have actually accessed the overdue books file.

_____ 7. You use a password you have discovered to get into the school's computer system and change your grade in algebra.

_____ 8. You and your friend are working together on a project for school. You both have the same program in your computers and decide to exchange disks once a week to transfer information from one computer to the other.

Answer the following questions on the lines provided.

9. How does a computer virus interfere with a computer? _____

_____

_____

10. How can you help to protect your computer system from an attack by a virus? _____

_____

_____

11. Why is hacking an invasion of privacy? _____

_____

_____

_____

_____

Chapter 24

REINFORCEMENT

● Radioactivity

Use the following section of the periodic table to complete the following.

55 Cs	56 Ba	71 Lu	72 Hf	73 Ta	74 W	75 Re	76 Os	77 Ir	78 Pt	79 Au	80 Hg	81 Tl	82 Pb	83 Bi	84 Po	85 At	86 Rn
87 Fr	88 Ra	103 Lr	104 Unq	105 Unp	106 Unh	107 Uns	108 Uno	109 Une									

57 La	58 Ce	59 Pr	60 Nd	61 Pm	62 Sm	63 Eu	64 Gd	65 Tb	66 Dy	67 Ho	68 Er	69 Tm	70 Yb
89 Ac	90 Th	91 Pa	92 U	93 Np	94 Pu	95 Am	96 Cm	97 Bk	98 Cf	99 Es	100 Fm	101 Md	102 No

1. Use a pencil to lightly shade in the boxes of the radioactive elements.

2. Draw an X through the boxes that represent synthetic elements.

3. How many of the radioactive elements are found in nature? _____

4. How many radioactive elements are made only in the laboratory? _____

5. What statement can you make about the relationship between atomic numbers and

   radioactivity? _____

The atomic mass of uranium is 92. The most stable isotope of uranium is uranium-238. The radioactive isotope of uranium is uranium-235. In the spaces provided, write the symbols for the nuclides of each isotope of uranium. Then, answer the questions.

Uranium-238	Uranium-235

6. How many neutrons does uranium-238 contain? _____

7. How many neutrons does uranium-235 contain? _____

Chapter 24

REINFORCEMENT

• Nuclear Decay

Element Z has a half-life of one week. Use the graph grid and the directions below to trace the decay of a 256-gram sample of element Z over a 10-week period. Each box on the grid represents one gram of element Z. After you complete each step, answer the question.

Week   **Directions and Questions**

1. Use a pencil to draw a large X through all of the boxes on the left half of the grid. How many grams of element Z decayed? _____

2. Use a different color pencil to draw a large X through 1/2 of the remaining boxes. How many grams of element Z remain after two weeks? _____

3. Use your pencil to shade 1/2 of the remaining boxes. How many grams of element Z are left? _____

4. Repeat step 3 using the colored pencil. How many grams of element Z remain?_____

5. Use a pencil to draw an X in 1/2 of the remaining boxes. How many grams of element Z remain? _____

6. Repeat step 5 using the colored pencil. How many grams of element Z remain?_____

7. Use your pencil to draw a circle in 1/2 of the remaining boxes. How many grams of element Z remain? _____

8. Repeat step 7 using the colored pencil. How many grams of element Z remain?_____

9. Shade in 1/2 of the remaining box with your pencil. How much of element Z remains? _____

10. Repeat step 9 using the colored pencil. How much of element Z remains? _____

On a separate sheet of graph paper, make a line graph or a bar graph that shows the decay of element Z over a 10-week period. Use your answers to questions 1–10 as your data.

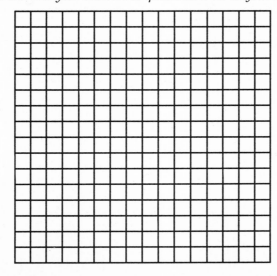

Chapter 24

REINFORCEMENT

Use with Text Pages 686–688

• Detecting Radioactivity

Determine whether the italicized term makes each statement true or false. If the statement is true, write the word "true" in the blank. If the statement is false, write in the blank the term that makes the statement true.

_____ 1. Radiation forms ions by removing *protons* from matter it passes through.

_____ 2. In a cloud chamber, *alpha* particles leave long, thin trails.

_____ 3. In a bubble chamber, a moving radioactive particle leaves ions behind causing the liquid to *boil* along the trail.

_____ 4. The simplest method of measuring radioactivity is to use *an electroscope.*

_____ 5. In a cloud chamber, *beta* particles leave short, thick trails.

_____ 6. Geiger counters are often used to test the radioactivity at job sites where workers are exposed to *radioactive* materials.

_____ 7. A radioactive particle moving through the air near an electroscope will cause the leaves of the electroscope to *move together.*

Match each type of radiation detector in Column II with its description in Column I. Write the letter of the correct term in the space provided.

Column I

_____ 8. Ionizing rays pass through a superheated liquid.

_____ 9. Ionizing rays pass through a supersaturated vapor.

_____ 10. loses charge in the presence of radiation

_____ 11. Radiation causes current to flow from a wire to produce a clicking sound or flashing light.

Column II

a. Geiger counter

b. electroscope

c. bubble chamber

d. cloud chamber

Chapter 24

REINFORCEMENT

• Nuclear Reactions

Use the diagram below to complete the following activities.

_____

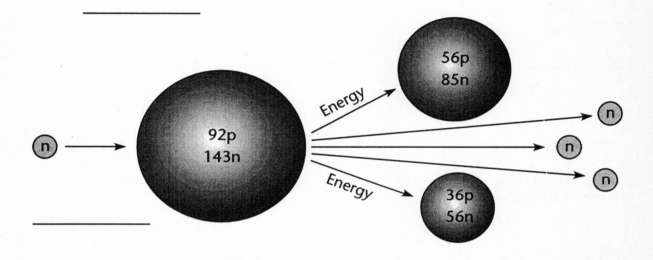

_____

1. The diagram shows two types of nuclear reactions: nuclear fission and nuclear fusion. Label the type of reaction shown in each diagram in the space provided.

2. Circle the letter of the equation that correctly explains the nuclear reaction shown in the top diagram.

   a. H-2 + H-2 → H-4   **b.** H-2 + H-2 → He-4   **c.** H-1 + H-1 → H-2   **d.** H-1 + H-1 → He-2

3. Circle the letter of the equation that correctly explains the nuclear reaction shown in the bottom diagram.

   a. 1 neutron + U-235 → Ba-141 + Kr-92 + 3 neutrons

   b. 1 neutron + U-238 → Ba-141 + Kr-92 + 4 neutrons

   c. Ba-141 + Kr-92 → U-235 + 3 neutrons

   d. Ba-142 + Kr-92 → U-238

4. What two elements are involved in the nuclear fusion reaction? _____

5. Label each atom in the fusion reaction with its correct symbol and isotope notation.

6. What three elements are involved in the fission reaction shown? _____

_____

7. Label each atom in the nuclear fission reaction with its chemical symbol and its correct isotope notation.

Chapter 24

REINFORCEMENT

• Using Nuclear Reactions in Medicine

On the lines provided, identify the radioisotope that would most likely be used to diagnose or treat a problem for the organ shown.

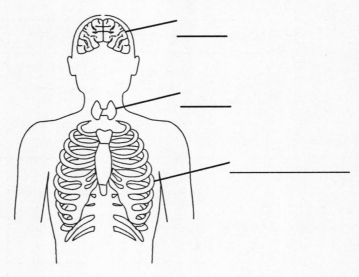

Answer the following questions on the lines provided.

1. The most stable form of iodine is iodine-126 with an atomic number of 53. How many

    neutrons does an atom of I-126 contain? _____

2. How does iodine-131 differ from iodine-126? _____

    _____

3. Cobalt usually has an atomic number of 27 and an atomic mass of 59. How does an atom of

    Co-60 differ from an atom of Co-59? _____

4. A stable technetium (Tc) atom has an atomic mass of 98 and an atomic number of 43. How

    many neutrons does an atom of technetium-99 have? _____

5. How many protons does Tc-99 have? _____

In the spaces provided below, write the symbols for the nuclides of the most common isotopes of iodine, cobalt, and gold. Then write the symbols for the nuclides of the radioisotopes of each element.

	Iodine	Cobalt	Gold
Common isotopes			
Radioisotopes			

Chapter 25

REINFORCEMENT

● Fossil Fuels

Complete the table below by placing a check mark (√) beneath the headings of the substances that have each characteristic described in the first column.

Characteristic	Petroleum	Natural Gas	Coal
1. is a fossil fuel			
2. forms from plants and animals			
3. forms only from plants			
4. is a solid			
5. is a liquid			
6. is a gas			
7. is made up of hydrocarbons			
8. is a source of energy			
9. is a nonrenewable resource			
10. is pumped from wells			
11. is separated using fractional distillation			
12. is also called crude oil			
13. is transported long distances through pipes			
14. is mined from Earth			
15. produces polluting substances when burned			
16. produces thermal energy when burned			
17. can be used to produce electricity			
18. is the least polluting fossil fuel			

Chapter 25

REINFORCEMENT

• Nuclear Energy

Place the following events describing the production of electrical energy from a nuclear fission reactor in the correct order. Write the numbers 1 (first) through 7 (last) in the spaces provided.

_____ **a.** Steam produced by boiling water causes the blades of a turbine to rotate.

_____ **b.** A neutron bombards a uranium-235 isotope.

_____ **c.** Thermal energy released by the reaction is added to water.

_____ **d.** Electricity from the generator is carried to the community through wires.

_____ **e.** A uranium-235 atom splits, producing two atoms with smaller nuclei, three neutrons, and thermal energy.

_____ **f.** The mechanical energy of the rotating turbine blades is transferred to an electric generator.

_____ **g.** Superheated water passes through a heat exchanger, where the thermal energy released boils a separate system of water to produce steam.

Answer the following questions about nuclear energy.

1. How does using nuclear energy harm the environment? _____

_____

2. How is using nuclear energy less harmful to the environment than using fossil fuels?

_____

_____

3. How does the half-life of a radioactive waste affect the type of container in which the waste

will be stored? _____

_____

_____

4. Why is nuclear fusion not currently used as an energy source on Earth?_____

_____

_____

5. How do the products of a fusion reaction differ from the products of a fission reaction?

_____

_____

Chapter 25

REINFORCEMENT

● Nuclear Waste and NIMBY

Circle the term or phrase in the parentheses that makes each statement true.

1. At present, proposals are being investigated to store high-level nuclear wastes in containers placed in (dried-up river beds, underground rock deposits).

2. The spent fuel from a nuclear reactor must be stored because it is (low-level, high-level) nuclear waste.

3. At present, military nuclear wastes are stored in (a single location, several locations) in the United States.

4. One reason spent fuel rods must be disposed of in durable containers is that they contain material with (very short, very long) half-lives.

5. Low-level nuclear wastes from medical processes are usually disposed of by being (buried in special landfills, burned).

6. Nuclear wastes are (radioactive by-products, unused nuclear materials) that remain after radioactive materials are used.

7. At present, a national storage site for high-level nuclear wastes has been seriously proposed near (Oak Ridge, Tennessee; Yucca Mountain, Nevada).

8. One recent proposal involved in disposing of nuclear wastes is to (seal them in ceramic glass globules, mix them with salt deposits).

9. The point of view that nuclear wastes should be stored but not in their immediate area is known as (NWPA, NIMBY).

10. If no new radioactive wastes were generated from today on, the problem of storage would (be eliminated, still remain).

11. One reason the federal government wants to establish a national, permanent storage site is that (some temporary sites have shown leakage, transportation problems would be reduced).

In the space provided, answer the following questions about a single, national, underground storage site.

12. What questions need to be answered before selecting a site? _____

_____

_____

_____

_____

13. What are the main points in favor of such a site? _____

_____

_____

_____

Chapter 25

REINFORCEMENT

● Alternative Energy Sources

Provide the information requested for each alternative energy source listed.

1. Biomasses

    a. What is biomass? _____

    b. How is biomass used? _____

    _____

2. Solar energy

    a. What is solar energy? _____

    b. What is passive solar heating? _____

    _____

    c. What is a photovoltaic cell? _____

3. Hydroelectricity

    a. What is hydroelectricity? _____

    _____

    b. What is one economic advantage to hydroelectricity? _____

    _____

4. Tidal energy

    a. What is tidal energy? _____

    b. Why is tidal energy a limited source of energy? _____

    _____

5. Wind energy

    a. What device is used to harness the energy in wind and convert it into electricity?

    _____

    b. Why is the wind an energy source with limited uses?_____

    _____

6. Geothermal energy

    a. What is geothermal energy? _____

    _____

    b. Where is geothermal energy used as a primary energy source?_____

Chapter 1

REINFORCEMENT ● Finding Out

Complete the following.

1. How does a problem differ from an exercise? **In an exercise, the steps required to find a solution usually are obvious. In a problem, the steps needed to find a solution may not be obvious.**

Identify the sense you would use to make each of the following observations.

sight — 2. the distance between two points

hearing — 3. the loudness of a stereo system

taste — 4. the saltiness of a stew

sight — 5. the number of students in a classroom

touch — 6. determining whether bathwater was too hot or too cold

taste or smell — 7. determining whether milk in a container has soured

taste — 8. the spiciness of a dinner

Identify the sense that each object listed is designed to help.

hearing — 9. hearing aid

sight — 10. microscope

touch — 11. thermometer

sight — 12. ruler

hearing — 13. stereo headphones

sight — 14. telescope

hearing — 15. stethoscope

Place the following terms in logical order by writing the numbers 1 through 4 in the spaces provided.

3 — 16. theory

4 — 17. scientific law

2 — 18. hypothesis

1 — 19. problem

20. What is an experiment? **a test of a hypothesis**

6

Chapter 1

REINFORCEMENT ● Science Is Everywhere

Use the definitions of pure science and technology listed below to decide whether the discovery described in each statement is an example of pure science or technology. Write a P for pure science or a T for technology in the space provided.

pure science: the study of a subject for the advancement of knowledge

technology: the application of scientific knowledge to improve the quality of life

P 1. Sarah observed that the shape of the moon seems to change slightly each night.

T 2. A scientist observed that coating glass with certain materials helped to prevent the glass from shattering.

T 3. A meteorologist discovered that a radar system developed to track the paths of airplanes could also be used to track the paths of storms.

P 4. While on a field trip, a geology student discovers a new kind of mineral.

T 5. A biologist discovered that bacteria could not grow in an environment where a certain kind of mold was present. The mold was later used to make the drug penicillin.

Place a check mark beside each item that is likely to be studied by a physical scientist.

√ 6. the energy given off by the sun

√ 7. which bones make up the human body

√ 8. the composition of the bones in the human body

√ 9. the temperature at which ice melts

√ 10. the substances that make up a drug

√ 11. the distance from the sun to Earth

___ 12. the fish population in a pond

√ 13. the speed at which electricity travels through a certain kind of wire

√ 14. how heat from the sun can be used to heat a home on Earth

___ 15. when the next bird migration occurs

___ 16. the amount of precipitation that falls in a desert

√ 17. the chemical makeup of a newly discovered mineral

5

Chapter 1
REINFORCEMENT

Getting Real with Special Effects

Write your answers to the following questions and activities in the spaces provided.

1. Why are special effects used in movies? **Special effects are used in movies to make**

   events seem more realistic. _____

2. Compare the composition of special-effects rocks and boulders used in old movies with the composition of those used in modern movies. How have new materials improved special-effects rocks? **In old movies special-effects rocks and boulders were made of papier**

   mâché. Today, polyurethane foam can be molded, cut, or carved into rocks and

   boulders, which can also be made from lightweight fiberglass. The new lightweight

   materials make the special-effects rocks and boulders look more realistic. _____

3. Compare the composition of special-effects glass used in old movies with the composition of glass used in modern movies. **In old movies, special-effects glass was called**

   "candy glass" because it was made from hardened sugar water. In modern movies

   glass is made from plastic. _____

4. How have new materials improved special-effects glass? **Modern plastic glass snaps to**

   pieces on impact and is more reliable than candy glass, which would melt from the heat

   of the movie lights or dissolve if gotten wet. _____

5. Describe the processes of claymation and go-motion. **Claymation is a process of animation**

   in which clay figures are photographed one frame at a time and the figures are moved

   slightly between frames. In the process of go-motion, computers move both the figures

   and the cameras simultaneously. _____

Chapter 1
REINFORCEMENT

Exploring Science

Complete the following.

1. Place the following in logical order by writing the numbers 1 through 5 in the spaces provided.

   5 a. analysis and conclusion   **4** d. observations and data

   2 b. hypothesis   **1** e. problem

   3 c. procedure

2. Is an experiment an example of an exercise or a problem? Why? **An experiment is made**

   up of a series of logical steps designed to provide a solution. Therefore, an experiment

   is more closely related to an exercise than a problem. _____

3. Why is a control important in an experiment? **A control shows that the result is related to**

   the condition being tested and not to some other condition. _____

4. Why is it important to follow all directions in an experiment carefully? **Following directions**

   helps to ensure the success of the experiment and helps to prevent the experimenter

   from being injured. _____

5. What two articles of clothing should always be worn when working in a science laboratory?

   safety glasses and a laboratory apron _____

Match each safety symbol in Column II with its description in Column I. Write the letter of the correct symbol in the blank on the left.

Column I	Column II
c 6. fire safety	a.
e 7. electrical safety	b.
a 8. sharp objects	c.
d 9. eye safety	d.
b 10. clothing protection	e.

Chapter 2

REINFORCEMENT

Use with Text Pages 38–47

• Using SI Units

1. Complete the table below by supplying the missing information.

Measurement	Base unit	Symbol
length	meter	m
mass	kilogram	kg
time	second	s
temperature	kelvin	K

In each of the following, circle the units that would most likely be used to express each kind of measurement. You may circle more than one answer for each item.

2. Volume of a solid: mL (m³) (cm³) L

3. Volume of a liquid: (mL) mg (cm³) L

4. Density of a material: g (g/cm³) (kg/m³) L

5. Temperature: °K (K) (°C) Kg

6. Mass: (kg) K cm³ (mg)

7. Time: kg K (s) mm

8. Length: K (km) (m) (cm)

For each pair of equations, write the letter of the equation that expresses an equal value.

_a_ 9. a. $1 \text{ L} = 1 \text{ dm}^3$ b. $1 \text{ L} = 1 \text{ cm}^3$

_a_ 10. a. $1 \text{ mL} = 1 \text{ cm}^3$ b. $1 \text{ cm}^3 = 1 \text{ L}$

_b_ 11. a. $0°C = -273 \text{ K}$ b. $0 \text{ K} = -273°C$

_b_ 12. a. $1 \text{ kg} = 100 \text{ g}$ b. $1000 \text{ g} = 1 \text{ kg}$

_a_ 13. a. $400 \text{ cm} = 4.0 \text{ m}$ b. $400 \text{ cm} = 0.40 \text{ m}$

_b_ 14. a. $1 \text{ dm} = 10 \text{ m}$ b. $1 \text{ dm} = 0.10 \text{ m}$

_a_ 15. a. $100°C = 373 \text{ K}$ b. $373 \text{ K} = 10°C$

16. Calculate the volume of the box in the diagram.

volume = 6 cm³

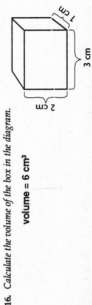

Chapter 2

REINFORCEMENT

Use with Text Pages 34–37

• Standards of Measurement

Fill in the missing information in the table below.

SI prefixes and their meanings

Prefix	Meaning
milli-	0.001
centi-	0.01
deci-	0.1
deka-	10
hecto-	100
kilo-	1000

Circle the larger unit in each pair of units.

1. millimeter (kilometer)

2. decimeter (dekameter)

3. (hectogram) decigram

4. (centimeter) millimeter

5. hectogram (kilogram)

6. In SI, the base unit of length is the meter. Use this information to arrange the following units of measurement in the correct order from smallest to largest. Write the number 1 (smallest) through 7 (largest) in the spaces provided.

  7   a. kilometer   6 e. hectometer

  2   b. centimeter   1 f. millimeter

  4   c. meter   3 g. decimeter

  5   d. dekameter

Use your knowledge of the prefixes used in SI to answer the following questions in the spaces provided.

7. One part of the Olympic games involves an activity called the decathlon. How many events do you think make up the decathlon? **A decathlon is made up of ten events.**

8. How many years make up a decade? **ten years**

9. How many years make up a century? **100 years**

10. What part of a second do you think a millisecond is? **0.001 second**

Chapter 2
REINFORCEMENT
● Graphing

Use the graphs below to answer the following questions.

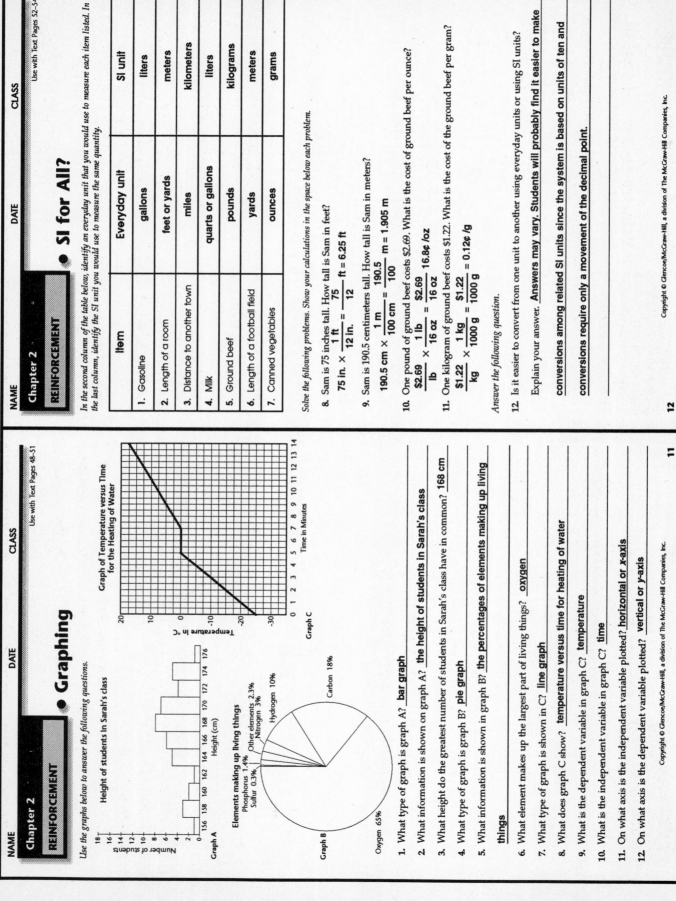

Height of students in Sarah's class

Graph A

Elements making up living things

Graph B

Oxygen 65%
Carbon 18%
Hydrogen 10%
Nitrogen 3%
Other elements 2.3%
Phosphorus 1.4%
Sulfur 0.3%

Graph of Temperature versus Time for the Heating of Water

Graph C

1. What type of graph is graph A? __bar graph__

2. What information is shown on graph A? __the height of students in Sarah's class__

3. What height do the greatest number of students in Sarah's class have in common? __168 cm__

4. What type of graph is graph B? __pie graph__

5. What information is shown in graph B? __the percentages of elements making up living things__

6. What element makes up the largest part of living things? __oxygen__

7. What type of graph is shown in C? __line graph__

8. What does graph C show? __temperature versus time for heating of water__

9. What is the dependent variable in graph C? __temperature__

10. What is the independent variable in graph C? __time__

11. On what axis is the independent variable plotted? __horizontal or x-axis__

12. On what axis is the dependent variable plotted? __vertical or y-axis__

11

Chapter 2
REINFORCEMENT
● SI for All?

In the second column of the table below, identify an everyday unit that you would use to measure each item listed. In the last column, identify the SI unit you would use to measure the same quantity.

	Item	Everyday unit	SI unit
1.	Gasoline	gallons	liters
2.	Length of a room	feet or yards	meters
3.	Distance to another town	miles	kilometers
4.	Milk	quarts or gallons	liters
5.	Ground beef	pounds	kilograms
6.	Length of a football field	yards	meters
7.	Canned vegetables	ounces	grams

Solve the following problems. Show your calculations in the space below each problem.

8. Sam is 75 inches tall. How tall is Sam in feet?

$$75 \text{ in.} \times \frac{1 \text{ ft}}{12 \text{ in.}} = \frac{75}{12} \text{ ft} = 6.25 \text{ ft}$$

9. Sam is 190.5 centimeters tall. How tall is Sam in meters?

$$190.5 \text{ cm} \times \frac{1 \text{ m}}{100 \text{ cm}} = \frac{190.5}{100} \text{ m} = 1.905 \text{ m}$$

10. One pound of ground beef costs $2.69. What is the cost of ground beef per ounce?

$$\frac{\$2.69}{\text{lb}} \times \frac{1 \text{ lb}}{16 \text{ oz}} = \frac{\$2.69}{16 \text{ oz}} = 16.8¢ /oz$$

11. One kilogram of ground beef costs $1.22. What is the cost of the ground beef per gram?

$$\frac{\$1.22}{\text{kg}} \times \frac{1 \text{ kg}}{1000 \text{ g}} = \frac{\$1.22}{1000 \text{ g}} = 0.12¢ /g$$

Answer the following question.

12. Is it easier to convert from one unit to another using everyday units or using SI units?
Explain your answer. __Answers may vary. Students will probably find it easier to make__ __conversions among related SI units since the system is based on units of ten and__ __conversions require only a movement of the decimal point.__

12

Chapter 3

REINFORCEMENT

● Motion and Speed

Sasha, Kim, and Barry decided to have a 10-km bicycle race after school. They asked the coach to show them how far 10 km was on the school track. They then had their race on the track. Their race results are shown on the time-distance graph below. Use this graph to fill in the table of race results, calculate average speeds, and answer the questions.

Distance (km) vs Time (minutes) — lines labeled Kim, Sasha, Barry

Race Results

Cyclist	Total distance	Total time	Average speed
Kim	10 km	50 mins	0.20 km/min
Sasha	10 km	55 mins	0.18 km/min
Barry	10 km	60 mins	0.17 km/min

1. Which cyclist kept a constant speed during the entire race? What was this speed? **Kim traveled 1 km every 5 minutes, therefore she traveled 0.20 km/min for the entire race.**

2. Which cyclist won the race? What was the winning time? **Kim won the race in 50 minutes.**

3. Which cyclist placed second in the race? What was second place time? **Sasha placed second in 55 minutes.**

4. Which cyclist placed last? What was last place time? **Barry placed last in 60 minutes.**

5. Which cyclist started off fastest? **Barry started off fastest. He traveled 5 km in 15 minutes. Kim traveled 5 km in 25 minutes, and Sasha traveled 5 km in 35 minutes.**

13

Chapter 3

REINFORCEMENT

● Velocity and Acceleration

The Car Race

The graph below represents three cars during the first minute of a race. Using the following information, draw another curve on the grid representing the motion of Car D.

Car D accelerates from a rest position at 0 seconds to a speed of 208 km/h at 5 seconds and maintains this speed for 5 seconds. The car decelerates to 32 km/h at 20 seconds. It then accelerates to a speed of 160 km/h at 30 seconds and maintains this speed for 5 seconds. Car D then decelerates to 112 km/h at 40 seconds, decelerates to 64 km/h at 50 seconds, and accelerates to 208 km/h at 55 seconds.

Use your graph to answer the following questions. Write your answers on the lines provided.

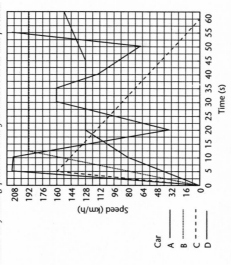

Speed (km/h) vs Time (s)

Car	
A	———
B	········
C	– – – –
D	———

1. Over which time period is Car B's acceleration the greatest? **0 – 12.5 sec**

2. What is Car B's speed at 10 seconds? **152 km/h**

3. When is Car B's acceleration equal to zero? **12.5 – 62.5 sec**

4. When is Car C's acceleration equal to zero? **at 5 seconds (this instant only)**

5. Which car(s) have a negative acceleration during the race? **C and D**

6. Which car has traveled the farthest at the end of one minute? **Car B**

   Students should note the area under each plot to determine this answer.

7. Which car may have had a reckless driver? Explain. **Car D. The graph shows Car D with positive and negative acceleration.**

8. Which car appears to have stalled? Explain. **Car C. The graph shows constant negative acceleration after 5 seconds.**

14

Chapter 3
REINFORCEMENT

● A Crash Course in Safety

Use the diagrams below to answer question 1.

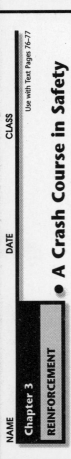
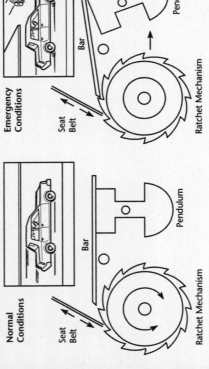

Normal Conditions

Seat Belt
Bar
Pendulum
Ratchet Mechanism

Emergency Conditions

Seat Belt
Bar
Pendulum
Ratchet Mechanism

Answer the following questions on the lines provided.

1. Why can you move freely in a seat belt under normal conditions but become "part" of the car upon collision? **Under normal conditions, the reel that the seat belt moves around remains free to move because the bar is out of the way of the ratchet mechanism on the reel. Upon collision, the pendulum moves forward and causes the bar to tip back and stop the reel via the ratchet mechanism. This locks the seat belt in place and allows the person wearing the seat belt to become "part" of the car.**

2. Inertia is the tendency of an object to resist any change in its motion. Explain how inertia affects a passenger in a head-on collision who is not wearing a seat belt. **Because of inertia, a passenger in a head-on car collision who is not wearing a seat belt will continue to move forward at the same speed that the car was traveling before the collision.**

3. Besides holding a person in place during a car collision, a seat belt serves another function. What is that function? **A seat belt not only holds a person in place, but also "gives," spreading out some of the force of the collision. Therefore, the force is not concentrated on one part of the person's body.**

Chapter 3
REINFORCEMENT

● Connecting Motion with Forces

Listed below are answers. Write a question for each answer. The first one has been done as an example.

1. push or pull   **What is a force?**

2. net force   **What kind of force always changes the velocity of an object?**

3. balanced forces   **What kind of forces are equal in size and opposite in directions?**

4. friction   **What is the force that opposes motion between surfaces that touch each other?**

5. inertia   **What is the tendency of an object to resist any change in its motion?**

6. Newton's first law of motion   **What law says that an object at a constant velocity keeps moving at that velocity unless a net force acts on it?**

Study the diagram below. Then answer the following questions by circling the letter that best answers each question.

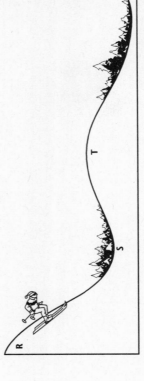

7. A person skis downhill from point R to point U. The speed of the skier increases in going from point R to point S because
   a. only balanced forces act on the skier.
   b. an unbalanced force acts on the skier. *(circled)*
   c. only inside forces act on the skier.
   d. no forces act on the skier.

8. The skier is able to coast between points S and T even though it is uphill because of
   a. gravity.
   b. centripetal force.
   c. cohesive force.
   d. inertia. *(circled)*

9. The force that opposes motion between the skier's skis and the surface of the snow is
   a. net.
   b. balanced.
   c. friction. *(circled)*
   d. inertia.

Chapter 4

REINFORCEMENT

Accelerated Motion

Use the equation F = m × a to solve the following problems. Show your calculations in the spaces provided.

1. How much force is needed to accelerate a 1000-kg car at a rate of 3 m/s²?

   $F = m \times a$ = 1000 kg × 3 m/s² = 3000 kg · m/s²
   F = 3000 N

2. If a 70-kg swimmer pushes off a pool wall with a force of 250 N, at what rate will the swimmer accelerate from the wall?

   $F = m \times a$
   250 N = 70 kg × a
   250 kg · m/s² = 70 kg × a

   $a = \dfrac{250 \text{ kg} \cdot \text{m/s}^2}{70 \text{ kg}} = 3.57$ m/s²

3. A weightlifter raises a 200-kg barbell with an acceleration of 3 m/s². How much force does the weightlifter use to raise the barbell?

   $F = m \times a$ = 200 kg × 3 m/s² = 600 kg · m/s²
   F = 600 N

4. A dancer lifts his partner above his head with an acceleration of 2.5 m/s². The dancer exerts a force of 200 N. What is the mass of the partner?

   $F = m \times a$
   200 N = m × 2.5 m/s²
   200 kg · m/s² = m × 2.5 m/s²

   $m = \dfrac{200 \text{ kg} \cdot \text{m/s}^2}{2.5 \text{ m/s}^2} = 80$ kg

Answer the following questions.

1. What does Newton's second law of motion state? <u>A net force acting on an object causes the object to accelerate in the direction of the force.</u>

2. What two factors affect the rate of acceleration of an object? <u>the size of the force exerted and the mass of the object</u>

3. At what rate does gravity cause objects to accelerate at sea level on Earth? <u>9.8 m/s²</u>

4. What is air resistance? <u>the force air exerts on a moving object</u>

5. What three factors affect the amount of air resistance on an object? <u>the speed, size, and shape of the object</u>

6. What is terminal velocity? <u>the highest velocity reached by a falling object</u>

Chapter 3

REINFORCEMENT

Gravity—A Familiar Force

Write answers to the following questions on the blank lines provided.

1. What is gravity? <u>Gravity is a force that every object in the universe exerts on every other object.</u>

2. What are two things that the amount of gravitational force between two objects depends on? <u>Earth has more mass their masses and the distance between them</u>

3. Why does Earth exert a stronger gravitational force than the moon? <u>Earth has more mass than the moon.</u>

4. If an object weighs 40 N on Earth, would it weigh more than 40 N on the moon? Explain your answer. <u>No. The moon exerts a smaller gravitational force than Earth. Weight is the measure of the force of gravity on an object; therefore an object that weighs 40 N on Earth would weigh less than 40 N on the moon.</u>

5. If an object has a mass of 26 g on Earth, would its mass be less than 26 g on the moon? Explain your answer. <u>No. Unlike weight, mass doesn't change with changes in gravity.</u>

Circle the picture in each set below that shows the greater gravitational force between the two objects.

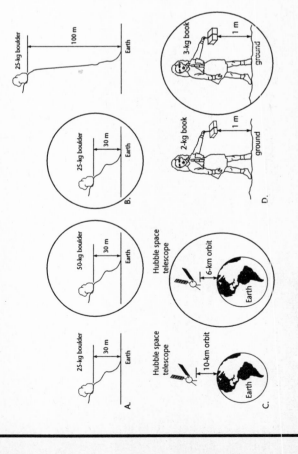

Chapter 4
REINFORCEMENT
Projectile and Circular Motion

Use the diagrams below to complete the following.

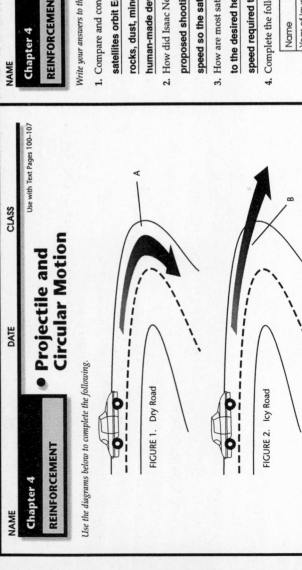

FIGURE 1. Dry Road

FIGURE 2. Icy Road

1. What force causes a moving object to move in a curved or circular path? __centripetal force__

2. What is the centripetal force that allows a car to move around a sharp curve in a roadway? __friction between the roadway and the car's tires__

3. Draw an arrow on the top diagram to show the direction the car will move when it reaches point A.

4. Draw an arrow on the bottom diagram to show the movement of the car if the centripetal force of the road and car is not enough to overcome the car's inertia when it reaches point B.

5. Explain how you know the car is accelerating when it reaches point A in the first diagram. __Acceleration is a change in the speed or direction of a moving object. Thus, when the car changes direction to go around the curve, it is accelerating.__

_____

_____

Chapter 4
REINFORCEMENT
Sending Up Satellites

Write your answers to the following questions and activities in the spaces provided.

1. Compare and contrast natural and artificial satellites. __Both natural satellites and artificial satellites orbit Earth or other planets. Natural satellites such as the moon are made of rocks, dust, minerals, and other materials that exist in nature. Artificial satellites are human-made devices that orbit Earth or other planets for specific purposes.__

2. How did Isaac Newton propose placing a cannonball in orbit as a satellite? __Isaac Newton proposed shooting a cannonball horizontally from a mountaintop and with enough speed so the satellite would stay in orbit and not fall back to Earth.__

3. How are most satellites placed in orbit? __A multistage rocket system boosts the satellite to the desired height of the orbit and then fires again to accelerate the satellite to the speed required to stay in orbit.__

4. Complete the following table about the first artificial Earth satellite.

Name	Sputnik
Year of launch	1957
Country of origin	Former Soviet Union
Mass	84 kg
Diameter	60 cm
Time for one revolution around Earth	90 minutes

5. How does a geostationary satellite differ from other satellites? __Unlike other satellites, a geostationary satellite is placed in orbit with a speed that matches the movement of Earth as it spins on its axis. As a result, a geostationary satellite appears to be stationary above a given location, while other satellites will appear to move.__

6. How are the tasks that geostationary satellites perform related to their geostationary orbits? __Because they are stationary relative to the rotating Earth, geostationary satellites can be used as receivers and transmitters to relay TV and radio signals and can be used to monitor weather patterns and ground temperature using different photographic techniques.__

7. What are some other tasks that satellites perform? __Satellites are used for military surveillance; for monitoring air and water pollution, food supplies, crop damage and water flows; and for studying many objects in outer space.__

8. What eventually happens to artificial satellites? __Air resistance gradually causes satellites to slow down, allowing Earth's gravity to pull them lower. As the satellites enter the denser part of Earth's atmosphere, they usually burn up in the extreme heat generated by atmospheric friction.__

Chapter 5
REINFORCEMENT
● Energy and Work

Place a plus (+) to the left of the statements that agree with what was said in the textbook. Place a minus (–) to the left of the statements that do not agree with the textbook, and write down the word or words that need to be changed and what they need to be changed to.

+   1. To a scientist, work is done when a force is exerted through a distance.

+   2. Any sample of matter has energy if it can produce a change in itself or in its surroundings.

+   3. A joule is equal to one newton meter.

–   4. According to the law of conservation of energy, energy can be created or destroyed under ordinary conditions. <u>Change *can* to *cannot*.</u>

+   5. For work to be done, motion must be in the direction of the applied force.

+   6. Mechanical energy is the total amount of kinetic and potential energy in a system.

–   7. A rock at the edge of a 200-m high cliff has more potential energy than an equal-sized rock at the edge of a 600-m high cliff. <u>Change *more* to *less*.</u>

+   8. The energy stored in foods, fuels, and dry cells is chemical potential energy.

+   9. When a force acts over a distance, the work done can be calculated using the formula $W = F \times d$.

Fill in the missing information. The chart below compares kinetic energy and gravitational potential energy.

Characteristic	Similarities and differences	
	Kinetic energy	Gravitational potential energy
Definition	energy of motion	energy of position
Units	joules	joules
Quantities involved	mass, velocity	weight, height

Chapter 4
REINFORCEMENT
● Action and Reaction

Use the diagram to complete the following.

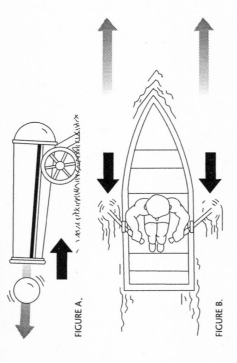

FIGURE A.

FIGURE B.

1. Draw an arrow on Figure A to show the direction the cannon will move when the cannonball is fired.

2. Draw arrows on Figure B to show the direction the oars must move to propel the boat forward.

3. Does the arrow you drew on Figure A represent an action force or a reaction force? <u>**reaction force**</u>

4. Does the arrow you drew on Figure B represent an action force or a reaction force? <u>**an action force**</u>

5. If the force which propels the cannonball forward is 500 N, how much force will move the cannon backward? Explain. <u>**The force will also be 500 N because action-reaction forces are equal and opposite.**</u>

Solve the following.

1. What is the momentum of a 2-kg toy truck that moves at 10 meters per second?

    $p = m \times v = 2 \text{ kg} \times 10 \text{ m/sec} = 20 \text{ kg} \cdot \text{m/s}$

2. What is the momentum of a 2000-kg truck that moves at 10 meters per second?

    $p = m \times v = 2000 \text{ kg} \times 10 \text{ m/s} = 20\,000 \text{ kg} \cdot \text{m/s}$

3. Which truck has more momentum? Why? <u>the 2000-kg truck because it has a greater mass</u>

Chapter 5
REINFORCEMENT

Use with Text Pages 134–137

Temperature and Heat

Determine whether the italicized term makes each sentence true or false. If the statement is true, write the word "true" in the blank. If the statement is false, write in the blank the term that makes the statement true.

__true__ 1. The particles that make up a sample of matter have *kinetic* energy.

__thermal energy__ 2. The more *mass* a material has, the greater its temperature.

__quickly__ 3. As the temperature of a material increases, the particles move more *slowly* and their average kinetic energy becomes greater.

__true__ 4. *Thermal* energy is the total energy of the particles in a material.

__heat__ 5. The energy that flows from something with a higher temperature to something with a lower temperature is *thermal energy*.

__joules__ 6. Heat is measured in *Celsius degrees*.

__true__ 7. Heat and *work* both involve transfers of energy.

__the same__ 8. At 22°C, a football has *less* thermal energy when it is sitting on the ground than when it is moving through the air.

__true__ 9. The kinetic and potential energy of the particles in a material determine its *thermal energy*.

__true__ 10. Different kinds of matter have *different* thermal energies.

__true__ 11. Heat energy flows from *warmer to cooler* materials.

__thermal energy__ 12. Mass, kind of matter, and the average kinetic energy of its particles determine the *temperature* of a material.

__true__ 13. Temperature is measured in *degrees*.

__slowly__ 14. The particles in a cup of cold coffee move more *quickly* than the particles in an equal-sized cup of hot coffee.

__work__ 15. Energy transferred when a force acts over a distance is *heat energy*.

Chapter 5
REINFORCEMENT

Use with Text Pages 138–140

Thermal Pollution: Waste You Can't See

Determine whether the italicized term makes each statement true or false. If the statement is true, write the word "true" in the space provided. If the statement is false, write in the blank the term that makes the statement true.

__waste__ 1. Much of the energy used in everyday life ends up as *useful* thermal energy that is given off to the surroundings.

__true__ 2. The heat removed from *air-conditioned* buildings and vehicles is released to the outside air.

__changes/warms__ 3. Thermal pollution occurs when waste heat significantly *cools* the temperature of the environment.

__true__ 4. Thermal pollution may be a problem in areas where power plants and factories use *water* to warm their buildings and equipment.

__water__ 5. A cooling tower is a device that is designed to cool *air*.

__true__ 6. The heat from warmed water dumped into a waterway *lowers* the dissolved oxygen content of the waterway.

__above__ 7. The temperature of the water discharged from an electric power plant typically ranges from 5 to 11 Celsius degrees *below* the temperature of the water-way that is receiving the discharge.

__true__ 8. A possible use of thermal energy in wastewater is to heat *greenhouses*.

Answer the following questions on the lines provided.

9. What ecological effects might dumping warmed water into a waterway have? __The heat from the warmer water accelerates chemical-biological processes and can alter the reproductive processes of the water plants and animals, causing major fish kills in extreme cases.__

10. How does a cooling tower function? __A cooling tower functions by cooling heated wastewater by using fans or through evaporation.__

Chapter 5

REINFORCEMENT

● Measuring Thermal Energy

Answer the following questions about specific heat and thermal energy on the lines provided.

1. Change in thermal energy can be calculated using the equation $Q = m \times \Delta T \times C_p$.

   a. In this equation, what does Q represent? __change in thermal energy__

   b. What does m represent? __the mass of the sample of matter__

   c. What does ΔT represent? __change in temperature__

   d. What does C_p represent? __specific heat__

   e. What does the symbol Δ mean? __change__

   f. Why is the symbol Δ used with T but not Q? __Change is included in Q, which is the__
      __variable for energy change.__

   g. In what units is T measured? __Celsius degrees__

   h. In what units is specific heat measured? __joules per kilogram per Celsius degree or__
      __J/kg · °C__

   i. In what unit is m measured? __kilograms__

2. What formula is used to calculate ΔT?

$$\Delta T = T_{final} - T_{initial}$$

3. Suppose that the temperature of 500 g of water changes from 25°C to 34°C over a period of two hours. How would you calculate the temperature change of the water?

$$\Delta T = T_{final} - T_{initial}$$
$$\Delta T = 34°C - 25°C$$
$$\Delta T = 9°C$$

4. Calculate the quantity of heat that must be transferred to 17.0 g of water to raise its temperature from 15°C to 17°C. Water has a specific heat of 4184 J/kg · °C.

$$Q = m \times \Delta T \times C_p$$
$$Q = 0.017 \text{ kg} \times 2°C \times 4184 \text{ J/kg} \cdot °C$$
$$Q = 142.46 \text{ J}$$

Chapter 6

REINFORCEMENT

● Thermal Energy on the Move

Determine whether the italicized term makes each statement true or false. If the statement is true, write the word "true" in the blank. If the statement is false, write in the blank the term that makes the statement true.

__good__   1. Materials that are poor conductors are *poor* insulators.

__conduction__   2. The transfer of energy through matter by direct contact of its particles is *convection*.

__radiation__   3. The transfer of energy in the form of invisible waves is *conduction*.

__true__   4. Solids usually conduct heat *better* than liquids and gases.

__true__   5. The R-value of insulation indicates its *resistance* to heat flow.

__true__   6. Air is a *poor* heat conductor.

__convection__   7. Wind and ocean currents are examples of *conduction* currents.

__convection__   8. Energy is usually transferred in fluids by *radiation*.

__true__   9. As water is heated, it expands, becomes *less* dense, and rises.

__more__   10. Dark-colored materials absorb *less* radiant energy than light-colored materials.

__absorbed__   11. Only radiant energy that is *reflected* is changed to thermal energy.

__more__   12. The higher the R-value of insulation the *less* resistant it is to heat flow.

Circle the object in each pair that will take in more heat. In the blank, explain why that object will take in more heat.

13. (a silver spoon,)
    a wooden log

__Silver is a better conductor of heat than wood.__

14. a white shirt,
    (a red shirt)

__Darker-colored materials absorb more heat than lighter-__
__colored materials.__

15. foil in the sun,
    (a sidewalk in the sun)

__Dull materials absorb more radiant energy than shiny__
__materials.__

16. (single-pane window,)
    double-pane window

__Air between the two panes of glass in the double-pane win-__
__dow acts as insulation.__

17. (R-5 insulation,)
    R-35 insulation

__Materials with a lower R-value are less resistant to heat flow.__

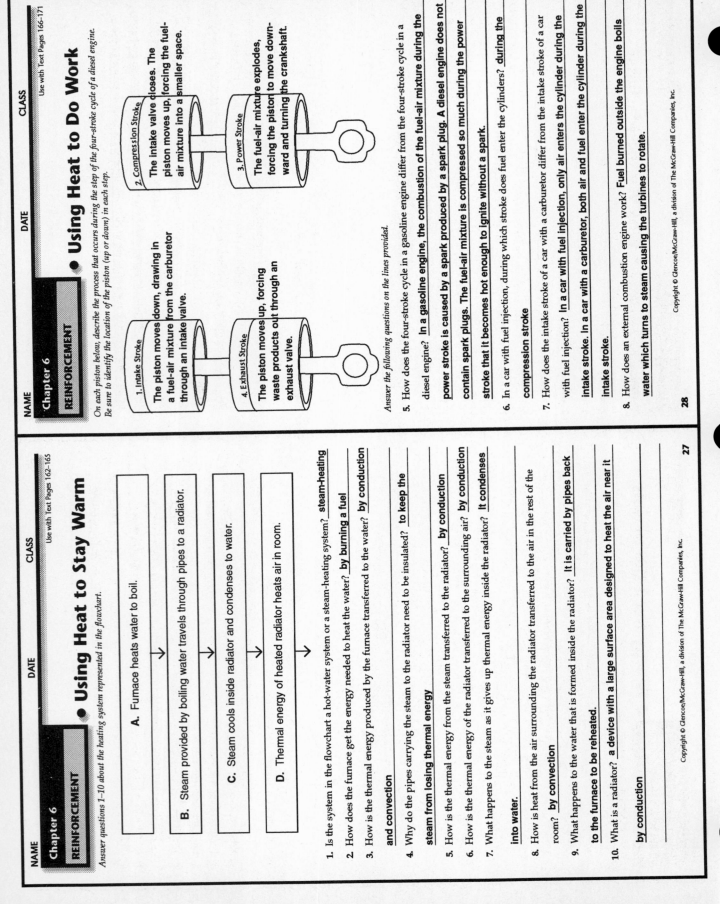

NAME   **DATE**   **CLASS**

Chapter 6

REINFORCEMENT ● **Using Heat to Stay Warm**

Use with Text Pages 162–165

Answer questions 1–10 about the heating system represented in the flowchart.

A. Furnace heats water to boil.

→

B. Steam provided by boiling water travels through pipes to a radiator.

→

C. Steam cools inside radiator and condenses to water.

→

D. Thermal energy of heated radiator heats air in room.

1. Is the system in the flowchart a hot-water system or a steam-heating system? **steam-heating**

2. How does the furnace get the energy needed to heat the water? **by burning a fuel**

3. How is the thermal energy produced by the furnace transferred to the water? **by conduction**
   and convection

4. Why do the pipes carrying the steam to the radiator need to be insulated? **to keep the**
   steam from losing thermal energy

5. How is the thermal energy from the steam transferred to the radiator? **by conduction**

6. How is the thermal energy of the radiator transferred to the surrounding air? **by conduction**

7. What happens to the steam as it gives up thermal energy inside the radiator? **It condenses**
   into water.

8. How is heat from the air surrounding the radiator transferred to the air in the rest of the
   room? **by convection**

9. What happens to the water that is formed inside the radiator? **It is carried by pipes back**
   to the furnace to be reheated.

10. What is a radiator? **a device with a large surface area designed to heat the air near it**
    by conduction

NAME   **DATE**   **CLASS**

Chapter 6

REINFORCEMENT ● **Using Heat to Do Work**

Use with Text Pages 166–171

On each piston below, describe the process that occurs during the step of the four-stroke cycle of a diesel engine. Be sure to identify the location of the piston (up or down) in each step.

1. Intake Stroke
The piston moves down, drawing in a fuel-air mixture from the carburetor through an intake valve.

2. Compression Stroke
The intake valve closes. The piston moves up, forcing the fuel-air mixture into a smaller space.

3. Power Stroke
The fuel-air mixture explodes, forcing the piston to move downward and turning the crankshaft.

4. Exhaust Stroke
The piston moves up, forcing waste products out through an exhaust valve.

Answer the following questions on the lines provided.

5. How does the four-stroke cycle in a gasoline engine differ from the four-stroke cycle in a
   diesel engine? **In a gasoline engine, the combustion of the fuel-air mixture during the**
   power stroke is caused by a spark produced by a spark plug. A diesel engine does not
   contain spark plugs. The fuel-air mixture is compressed so much during the power
   stroke that it becomes hot enough to ignite without a spark.

6. In a car with fuel injection, during which stroke does fuel enter the cylinders? **during the**
   compression stroke

7. How does the intake stroke of a car with a carburetor differ from the intake stroke of a car
   with fuel injection? **In a car with fuel injection, only air enters the cylinder during the**
   intake stroke. In a car with a carburetor, both air and fuel enter the cylinder during the
   intake stroke.

8. How does an external combustion engine work? **Fuel burned outside the engine boils**
   water which turns to steam causing the turbines to rotate.

Chapter 7

REINFORCEMENT

• Why We Use Machines

In the spaces provided, write the equation you would use to calculate each of the following. Use the appropriate symbols in your equations.

1. work $W = F \times d$

2. work input $W_{in} = F_e \times d_e$

3. work output $W_{out} = F_r \times d_r$

4. mechanical advantage $MA = F_r/F_e$

5. work input and work output in an ideal machine $W_{in} = W_{out}$

Use the equations you wrote above to solve the following problems. Be sure to use the appropriate units in your answers.

6. A carpenter used a claw hammer to pull a 2-cm nail out of a piece of wood. The nail had a resistance of 1500 N. The carpenter exerted a force of 250 N.

   a. What is the work output of the hammer on the nail?
   $W = F \times d = 1500\ N \times 2\ cm = 1500\ N \times 0.02\ m = 30\ Nm = 30\ J$

   b. What was the mechanical advantage of the hammer?

   $$MA = \frac{F_r}{F_e} = \frac{1500\ N}{250\ N} = 6$$

   c. If work input equals work output, what is the work input by the carpenter?   _____ 30 J

Answer the following questions with complete sentences.

7. What are two ways that a machine makes work easier?   A machine makes work easier by changing the size or direction of the force, or both.

8. How does a hammer used to pull a nail from a board change the direction of the force?   When you push down on the handle of the hammer, the claw of the hammer pulls up on the nail.

9. When you use a hammer to drive a nail into a piece of wood, are you changing the size or the direction of the force?   A hammer used to drive a nail into a piece of wood changes the size of the force because the hammer allows the user to apply more force to the head of the nail than could be done by trying to push the nail into the wood with one's fingers.

Chapter 6

REINFORCEMENT

• Energy from the Oceans

Determine whether the italicized term makes each statement true or false. If the statement is true, write the word "true" in the space provided. If the statement is false, write in the blank the term that makes the statement true.

__areas__   1. Because the oceans have large surface *currents* and great depths, they can absorb radiant energy from the sun and store it as thermal energy.

__mechanical__   2. Several hydroelectric plants are using the *thermal* energy of tides to rotate turbines and generate electricity.

__true__   3. There can be more than 20ºC difference between warm surface water and cold bottom waters in tropical and *subtropical* regions.

__heat__   4. Ocean thermal energy conversion (OTEC) is a process that uses *electric* engines to convert differences in ocean water temperature into mechanical energy to drive turbines.

__true__   5. Present OTEC plants have *low* efficiencies because large amounts of water must be pumped from ocean depths.

In the spaces provided, write your answers to the following questions and activities relating to the OTEC heat engine shown in Figure 6-1.

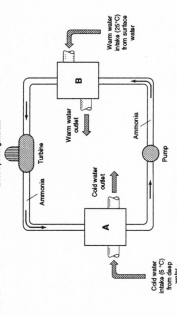

6. Is the ammonia passing through the pump gas or liquid?   liquid

7. Is the ammonia passing through the turbine gas or liquid?   gas

8. What happens to the ammonia in chamber A?   The ammonia vapor condenses.

9. For the turbine to operate, the ammonia passing through it must have what type of energy?   mechanical/kinetic energy

10. Why must the water passing around chamber A be cold (5ºC)?   The water must be cold so that it absorbs thermal energy from the ammonia vapor causing it to condense.

11. What happens to the ammonia in chamber B?   The ammonia liquid evaporates.

12. Why must the water passing around chamber B be warm (25ºC)?   The water must be warm so that it can transfer thermal energy to the ammonia liquid so that the ammonia evaporates.

Chapter 7
REINFORCEMENT

• The Simple Machines

Match each simple machine in Column II to its description in Column I. Write the letter of the simple machine in the blank on the left.

Column I | **Column II**

d 1. bar that is free to pivot about a fixed point — a. wheel and axle

e 2. an inclined plane with one or two sloping sides — b. inclined plane

f 3. grooved wheel with a rope running along the groove — c. gear

a 4. two wheels of different sizes that rotate together — d. lever

b 5. sloping surface used to raise objects — e. wedge

c 6. wheel with teeth along its circumference — f. pulley

g 7. inclined plane wrapped in a spiral around a cylindrical post — g. screw

Classify each type of simple machine as either a lever or an inclined plane by writing its name in the proper column of the table.

8. Levers	9. Inclined Planes
pulley	wedge
wheel and axle	screw
lever	inclined plane
gear	

Calculate the mechanical advantage for each of the following simple machines.

10. A person uses a crow bar to move a rock that weighs 200 N. The effort arm is 50 cm long. The resistance arm is 20 cm long.

$$MA = \frac{L_e}{L_r} = \frac{50 \text{ cm}}{20 \text{ cm}} = 2.5$$

11. A painter uses a fixed pulley to raise a 1-kg can of paint a distance of 10 m. The MA of a fixed pulley is always one. Students can demonstrate this by using the following equation:

$$MA = \frac{L_e}{L_r} = \frac{10 \text{ m}}{10 \text{ m}} = 1$$

12. A screwdriver with a 1-cm shaft and a 4-cm handle is used to tighten a screw.

$$MA = \frac{r_w}{r_a} = \frac{4 \text{ cm}}{1 \text{ cm}} = 4$$

Chapter 7
REINFORCEMENT

• Mending with Machines

Determine whether the italicized term makes each statement true or false. If the statement is true, write the word "true" in the space provided. If the statement is false, write in the blank the term that makes the statement true.

brain 1. Some parts of your body act as simple machines and are controlled by nerve impulses from your *eyes.*

true 2. Organs such as kidneys and hearts can be *transplanted* from one person to another.

Artificial 3. *Natural* replacement parts for human bodies are called prostheses.

bionics 4. The science of designing artificial replacements for body parts is called *robotics.*

true 5. In the 1700s, Volta observed that *muscles* could be affected by electric shocks.

Use the terms in the box to fill the blanks to the right of the letters below that correspond to the labeled parts of the prosthesis shown in Figure 7-1.

microprocessor	nerve interface	radio transmitter	stump
nerve	prosthesis	receiver	touch sensors

6. a. **nerve**   c. **radio transmitter**   e. **prosthesis**   g. **microprocessor**

   b. **nerve interface**   d. **stump**   f. **receiver**   h. **touch sensors**

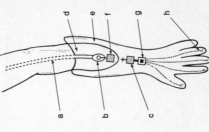

Figure 7-15.

Answer the following questions with complete sentences.

7. How might the prosthesis shown in Figure 7-15 allow an amputee to feel sensations such as pressure and texture? **Sensors and a power source capable of generating artificial neural signals would be placed in the prosthesis, and the sensors would be connected to the remaining healthy portion of the natural arm's nerve to carry neural impulses to the brain.**

8. How might brain-to-computer interfaces help a person regain the use of a dysfunctional limb? **Electrodes collect signals from brain neurons. The signals operate a prosthesis.**

Chapter 7

REINFORCEMENT ● Using Machines

Use the formula, efficiency = (W_{out} / W_{in}) × 100%, to calculate the efficiency of each of the following machines.

1. A 600-N box is pushed up a ramp that is 2 m high and 5 m long. The person pushing the box exerts a force of 300 N. What is the efficiency of the ramp?

$$\text{efficiency} = \frac{W_{out}}{W_{in}} \times 100\% = \frac{F \times d_r}{F_e \times d_e} \times 100\%$$

$$= \frac{600\text{ N} \times 2\text{ m}}{300\text{ N} \times 5\text{ m}} \times 100\% = \frac{1200\text{ Nm}}{1500\text{ Nm}} \times 100\%$$

$$= 0.8 \times 100\% = 80\%$$

2. A person uses a fixed pulley to raise a 75-N object 40 m. The force exerted on the object is 120 N. What is the efficiency of the pulley?

$$\text{efficiency} = \frac{W_{out}}{W_{in}} \times 100\% = \frac{F_r \times d_r}{F_e \times d_e} \times 100\%$$

$$= \frac{75\text{ N} \times 40\text{ m}}{120\text{ N} \times 40\text{ m}} \times 100\%$$

$$= 0.625 \times 100\% = 62.5\%$$

Use the formula, power = work/time to calculate the power required in each of the following.

3. A weightlifter lifts a 1250-N barbell 2 m in 3 s. How much power was used to lift the barbell?

$$W = F \times D \qquad\qquad P = \frac{W}{T} = \frac{2500\text{ J}}{3\text{ s}}$$

$$= 1250\text{ N} \times 2\text{ m} \qquad\qquad = 833\text{ J/s}$$

$$= 2500\text{ N} \cdot \text{m} = 2500\text{ J} \qquad\qquad = 833\text{ watts}$$

4. A crane lifts a 35 000-N steel girder a distance of 25 m in 45 s. How much power did the crane require to lift the girder? Write your answer in kilowatts.

$$P = \frac{W}{t} = \frac{F \times d}{t} = \frac{35\,000\text{ N} \times 25\text{ m}}{45\text{ s}}$$

$$= \frac{875\,000\text{ J}}{45\text{ s}} = 19\,444.444\text{ watts}$$

$$= 19.44\text{ kilowatts}$$

Chapter 8

REINFORCEMENT ● Matter and Temperature

Answer the following questions in the blanks provided. Use complete sentences where appropriate.

1. What are the three common states of matter?

a. __solids__   b. __liquids__   c. __gases__

What is the fourth state of matter? __plasma__

2. Complete the following chart describing the shape and volume for the three common states of matter.

State of Matter	Volume	Shape
solid	definite	definite
liquid	definite	indefinite
gas	indefinite	indefinite

How does the fourth state of matter differ from the other three? __Like a gas, plasma has no__ __definite volume or shape, but it differs in that it consists of charged particles.__

3. Use the kinetic theory of matter to explain the behavior of the three common states of matter. __In solids, particles have enough energy to vibrate in place, but not enough to move__ __from one place to another. Thus, the material keeps its shape as well as its volume. In__ __liquids, particles have enough energy to both vibrate and to slip over one another, but__ __they still stay close together. Thus, the material keeps its volume but is able to flow__ __from one place to another. In gases, particles have enough energy to move freely and__ __escape the attraction of one another. Particles move in straight lines throughout the__ __container. Thus, gases have no definite shape and no definite volume.__

4. In general, when you heat a substance, it expands. This phenomenon is called thermal expansion. Use the kinetic theory to explain thermal expansion. Give an example of thermal expansion that you have observed. __As a substance is heated, the particles that make up__ __the substance acquire more energy. When this happens, the particles move faster and__ __bounce harder off one another. Thus, the particles move farther apart and the material__ __expands. Accept any reasonable example, such as a balloon will expand and may even__ __break if it is left in a closed car on a hot summer day.__

Chapter 8

REINFORCEMENT

Use with Text Pages 224–227

● Changes in State

Look carefully at the graph. It was drawn from the data collected when a substance was heated at a constant rate. To heat at a constant rate means to add heat evenly as time passes. Use the graph to complete the paragraphs that follow.

At the start of observations, Point A, the substance exists in the **solid** state. The temperature at this point is **10°C** . As energy is **absorbed** , the temperature of the substance rises at a constant rate for two minutes. At Point B, the temperature is **50°C** , and the solid begins to **melt** . The temperature remains constant until the change from solid to **liquid** is complete. It has taken three minutes to add enough energy to melt the solid completely. From Point C to Point D, the substance is in the **liquid** state. Its temperature rises at a constant rate to **110°C** . The temperature remains constant while the liquid changes to a **gas** . At Point E, the substance exists as a **gas** . Its temperature rises **evenly** as energy is added.

When the gaseous substance is allowed to cool, it **releases** energy. The cooling curve will be the reverse of the warming curve. Energy will be released as the substance changes from a **gas** to a **liquid** and also from a **liquid** to a **solid** . The amount of energy released during condensation will be the same as the amount **absorbed** during vaporization.

Chapter 8

REINFORCEMENT

Use with Text Pages 222–223

● Fresh Water: Will There Be Enough?

Write definitions for the following terms in the space provided.

1. fresh water **Fresh water is water that is not salty and makes up only 0.75% of the water available on Earth in the liquid state.**

2. polluted water **Polluted water is water that contains such high levels of unwanted materials that it is unacceptable for drinking or other specific purposes.**

3. thermal pollution **Thermal pollution is a form of pollution that involves the heating of water in rivers and lakes to the point that the temperature of the water is harmful to organisms.**

Answer the following questions on the lines provided.

4. In what ways can groundwater be polluted by farms? **Fertilizers, pesticides, and herbicides may enter the groundwater.**

5. What can you do daily in your own life to save water and reduce water pollution? **Answers will vary but may include: not let water run when it is not necessary; use biodegradable soaps and detergents; dispose of substances in a safe way, such as taking used motor oil to your local filling station for disposal instead of dumping it on the ground or down the drain.**

6. Using Table 8-1 in your textbook, explain why self-service car washes are permitted to stay open when city officials forbid home car washing because of a drought? **Washing a car at a self-service car wash only uses 5–10 gallons of water. Washing a car at home with a hose can use up to 150 gallons of water.**

Chapter 8

REINFORCEMENT ● Behavior of Gases

Write the definitions for the following terms in the spaces provided.

1. Boyle's law __Boyle's law states that if you decrease the volume of a container of gas,__

   __the pressure of the gas will increase, provided the temperature does not change.__

2. Charles's law __Charles's law states that the volume of a gas increases with increasing__

   __temperature, provided the pressure does not change.__

3. pressure __Pressure is the amount of force exerted per unit of area.__

4. absolute zero __Absolute zero is the theoretical temperature at which a gas would__

   __have a volume of zero. This temperature is –273°C, or 0 K.__

Explain what will happen in each of the following cases.

5. If the temperature remains constant, what will happen to the pressure of a gas if you

   decrease the volume of the container that holds the gas? __The pressure will increase.__

6. If the volume of a container of gas remains constant, what will happen to the pressure of a

   gas if you increase temperature? __The pressure will increase.__

Answer the following questions regarding temperature.

7. On the Kelvin scale, what is the freezing point of water? __273 K__

8. On the Kelvin scale, what is the boiling point of water? __373 K__

9. On the Celsius scale, what are the freezing and boiling points of water?

   __freezing point = 0°C, boiling point = 100°C__

Chapter 8

REINFORCEMENT ● Uses of Fluids

Determine whether the italicized term makes each statement true or false. If the statement is true, write the word "true" in the blank. If the statement is incorrect, write in the blank the term that makes the statement true.

__gas__   1. A fluid is a liquid or a *solid*.

__an upward__   2. Buoyancy is the ability of a fluid to exert a *downward* force on an object immersed in it.

__less than__   3. If the buoyant force on an object is *greater than* the weight of the object, the object will sink.

__true__   4. The buoyant force on an object in a fluid is *equal to* the weight of the fluid displaced by the object.

__Pascal's__   5. *Archimedes'* principle states that pressure applied to a fluid is transmitted unchanged throughout the fluid.

__decreases__   6. As the velocity of a fluid increases, the pressure exerted by the fluid *increases*.

__true__   7. The Venturi effect describes how fluids flow *faster* when forced to flow through narrow spaces.

Answer the following questions on the lines provided.

8. A hydraulic machine can be used to lift extremely heavy objects. Why is the fluid in the hydraulic machine a liquid rather than a gas? __The liquid cannot be further compressed__ __and thus can be used to transfer pressure effectively throughout the system.__ __Because a gas is highly compressible, it would not be suitable for use in this device.__

9. A block of wood is floating in water. The weight of the part of the block above water is one-third of the total weight of the block. What is the weight of the water displaced by the block of wood? Explain your answer in terms of Archimedes' principle. __The weight of__ __the water is equal to the weight of the portion of the wood block that is submerged.__ __According to Archimedes' principle, the buoyant force on an object in a fluid is equal__ __to the weight of the fluid displaced by the object.__

10. A passenger jet in the air increases its speed. Does the downward force of air on the top of the wings increase or decrease? Does the net lifting force of the air on the wings increase or decrease? Explain your answer. __The downward force decreases. The lifting force__ __increases. Bernoulli's principle states that as the velocity of a fluid increases, the__ __pressure exerted by the fluid decreases.__

Chapter 9
REINFORCEMENT

Composition of Matter

Use with Text Pages 246–251

Use the words listed below to correctly complete the concept map.

atoms (different)	atoms (same)	colloids	fog
gold	iron	mixtures	muddy water
oxygen	salt	smoke	soft drinks
solutions	substances	suspensions	syrup
vinegar	water	whipped cream	

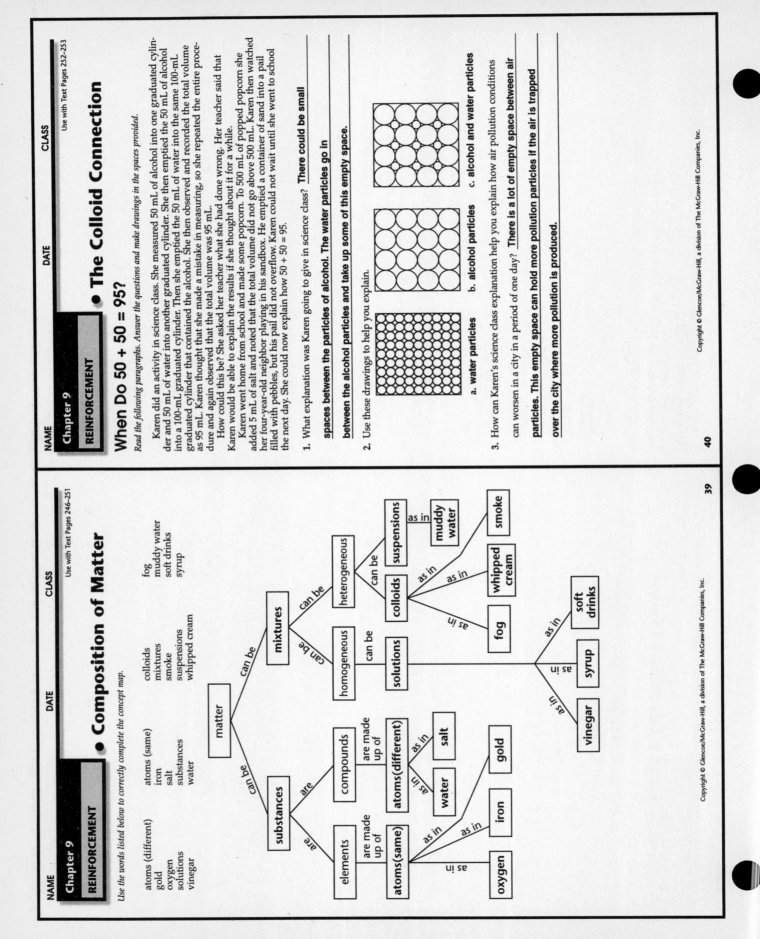

Chapter 9
REINFORCEMENT

The Colloid Connection

Use with Text Pages 252–253

When Do 50 + 50 = 95?

Read the following paragraphs. Answer the questions and make drawings in the spaces provided.

Karen did an activity in science class. She measured 50 mL of alcohol into one graduated cylinder and 50 mL of water into another graduated cylinder. She then emptied the 50 mL of alcohol into a 100-mL graduated cylinder. Then she emptied the 50 mL of water into the same 100-mL graduated cylinder that contained the alcohol. She then observed and recorded the total volume as 95 mL. Karen thought that she made a mistake in measuring, so she repeated the entire procedure and again observed that the total volume was 95 mL.

How could this be? She asked her teacher what she had done wrong. Her teacher said that Karen would be able to explain the results if she thought about it for a while.

Karen went home from school and made some popcorn. To 500 mL of popped popcorn she added 5 mL of salt and noted that the total volume did not go above 500 mL. Karen then watched her four-year-old neighbor playing in his sandbox. He emptied a container of sand into a pail filled with pebbles, but his pail did not overflow. Karen could not wait until she went to school the next day. She could now explain how 50 + 50 = 95.

1. What explanation was Karen going to give in science class? There could be small spaces between the particles of alcohol. The water particles go in between the alcohol particles and take up some of this empty space.

2. Use these drawings to help you explain.

a. water particles   b. alcohol particles   c. alcohol and water particles

3. How can Karen's science class explanation help you explain how air pollution conditions can worsen in a city in a period of one day? There is a lot of empty space between air particles. This empty space can hold more pollution particles if the air is trapped over the city where more pollution is produced.

Chapter 9
REINFORCEMENT

● Describing Matter

Use with Text Pages 254–261

Analogies

Below are two sets of words. Complete the second set by choosing a word from those listed below the blank. The two words must be related in the same way as the first set of words.

EXAMPLE
letter:envelope::pillow:[case]
case, sheet, soft, bed

1. steam:water::water: **ice**
   heat, molecules, ice, matter

2. solid:melting::liquid: **vaporizing**
   condensing, heating, mixing, vaporizing

3. physical:chemical::size: **burning**
   burning, taste, solubility, acid

4. liquid:vaporizing::solid: **melting**
   melting, freezing, decomposing, evaporating

5. iron:rust::silver: **tarnish**
   reaction, oxygen, tarnish, water

6. chemical:rust::physical: **condensation**
   compound, condensation, solid, change

7. element:compound::oxygen: **water**
   water, hydrogen, matter, mixture

8. compound:mixture::chemical: **physical**
   physical, separation, property, gas

9. hydrogen:water::carbon: **carbon dioxide**
   carbon dioxide, graphite, coal, gas

10. solid:steel::gaseous: **air**
    coal, air, water, gasoline

11. burning:candle::corrosion: **copper**
    vaporization, physical property, copper, mixture.

Chapter 10
REINFORCEMENT

● Structure of the Atom

Use with Text Pages 270–275

Use the clues to complete the puzzle.

Across

3. Scientist who developed the planetary model of the atom
7. Element 105
11. Region surrounding the nucleus which is occupied by electrons
13. Atomic number of fluorine (spelled out)
14. Center of atom
15. Symbol for sodium
16. Symbol for silver
18. Fe is the symbol.
21. Name of element used in fluorescent signs
22. Atom of an element with a different number of neutrons
23. Sum of protons and neutrons
25. Only element with atoms which do not have neutrons

Down

1. Element often made into electrical wire
2. Number of protons in an atom
4. Name of element whose symbol is Ru
5. Negatively charged particle
6. Mixture of mostly nitrogen and oxygen
8. 1/12 the mass of a carbon-12 atom
9. Helps us understand something that we cannot see directly
10. These are like shelves where electrons can be found.
12. Equal in number to the number of protons
14. A particle with approximately the same mass as a proton
17. Element used in balloons
19. Element name of radioactive gas that can accumulate in houses
20. Positively charged particle in nucleus
24. The building block of matter

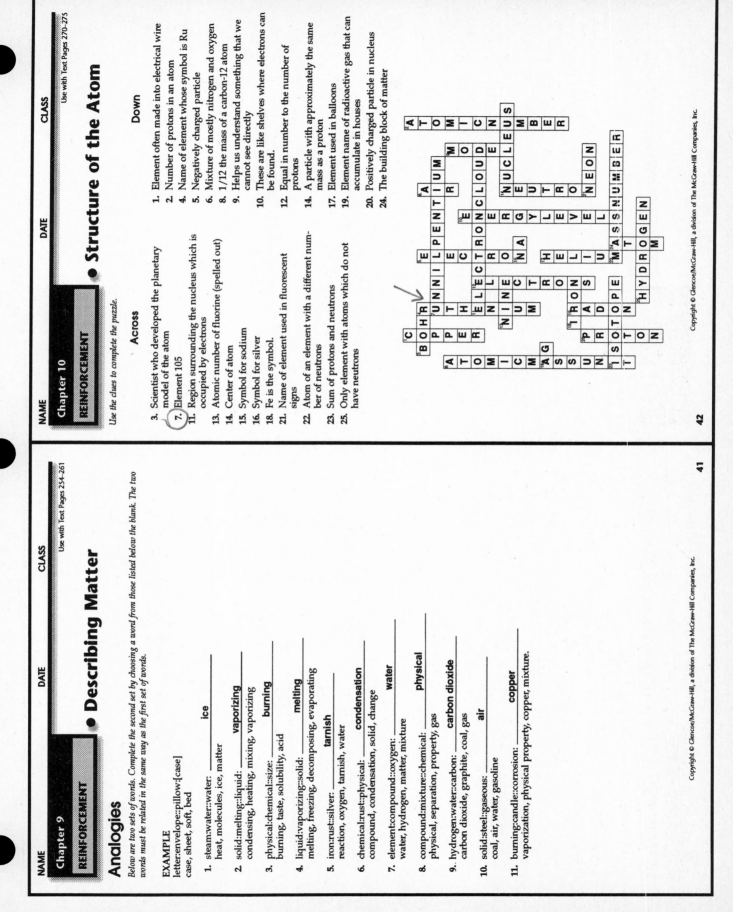

Chapter 10

REINFORCEMENT

● Masses of Atoms

Isotopes

Answer the following questions on the lines provided.

1. Define isotopes. Isotopes are atoms of the same element that differ only in the number of neutrons in their nucleus.
_____

2. How many isotopes can an element have? It depends on the element. Some elements have only one isotope and others have many. In addition to the isotopes that occur in nature, scientists have been able to produce other isotopes artificially in the laboratory.
_____

3. What is the average atomic mass of an element? The average atomic mass of an element is the average mass of the mixture of its isotopes.
_____
_____

4. Compare and contrast the atomic structure of the chlorine-35 and chlorine-37 isotopes. The two chlorine isotopes have the same number of protons in their nuclei and the same number of electrons around their nuclei. However, chlorine-37 has two more neutrons in its nucleus than does chlorine-35.
_____
_____

5. Suppose that a newly discovered element called centium has three isotopes that occur in nature. These are centium-200, centium-203, and centium-209. Assume that these isotopes occur in equal amounts in nature. What will be the average atomic mass of this element? Because these isotopes occur in equal parts in nature, the average atomic mass will be simply an average of the three atomic masses. Therefore, the average atomic mass will be 204 μ.
_____
_____

Chapter 10

REINFORCEMENT

● Smaller Particles of Matter

Answer each of the following questions with one or two sentences.

1. What is a quark? How many types of quarks are known? A quark is a subatomic particle that makes up protons and neutrons. So far, experiments have shown evidence for six types of quarks.
_____

2. How can scientists study the inner structure of the atom? Electric and magnetic fields are used to accelerate, focus, and then collide fast-moving electrons and protons.
_____

3. Describe the Tevatron's purpose and how it works. The purpose of the Tevatron is to study the inner structure of the atom. Information about this structure is revealed by the collision of fast-moving protons produced in electric and magnetic fields that accelerate and focus the protons.
_____
_____
_____

Chapter 11

REINFORCEMENT

● Why Atoms Combine

Each statement below contains a pair of terms or phrases in parentheses. Circle the term or phrase that makes each statement true.

1. Most of the matter around you is in the form of (elements, (compounds)).

2. The properties of a compound are (the same as, (different from)) the properties of the elements that make up the compound.

3. Na and Cl are ((chemical symbols), chemical formulas).

4. NaCl and NaOH are (chemical symbols, (chemical formulas)).

5. H_2O is the formula for (salt, (water)).

6. In the formula H_2O, the number 2 is a ((subscript), superscript).

7. In the formula HCl, the ratio of hydrogen atoms to chlorine atoms is ((1:1), 2:1).

8. The number 2 in the formula H_2O tells you that each unit of this compound contains ((2 hydrogen atoms), 2 oxygen atoms).

9. If a symbol in a chemical formula does not have a subscript after it, a unit of that compound contains (0 atoms, (1 atom)) of that element.

10. In the formula Fe_2O_3, the ratio of iron atoms to oxygen atoms is (3:2, (2:3)).

11. An atom is chemically stable if its outer energy level ((is filled with), contains no) electrons.

12. For atoms of most elements, the outer energy is filled when it has ((3 8)) electrons.

13. The noble gases do not readily form compounds because they ((are), are not) chemically stable.

14. A chemical bond is a ((force), chemical) that holds together the atoms in a compound.

15. Chemical bonds form when atoms lose, gain, or ((share), multiply) electrons.

Complete the table below by using the formula of each compound to identify the elements that each compound contains and the ratios of those elements. The first one has been done for you as an example.

Formula	Elements in compound	Ratios
H_2O	hydrogen, oxygen	2:1
NaOH	**nitrogen, oxygen, hydrogen**	1:1:1
NaCl	**sodium, chlorine**	1:1
NH_3	**nitrogen, hydrogen**	1:3
H_2SO_4	**hydrogen, sulfur, oxygen**	2:1:4
SiO_2	**silicon, oxygen**	1:2

Chapter 10

REINFORCEMENT

● The Periodic Table

You will need a scientist's patience to find the names of the 70 elements hidden in the grid. The Lanthanides and the Actinides have been excluded. The same letters may appear in more than one element name. Draw a line through the letters that correctly spell the name of an element.

Complete the following paragraphs about the periodic table by filling each blank with the correct word.

In the modern periodic table, elements are listed by increasing ____**atomic number**____.

Each box represents an ____**element**____. A box contains the name, atomic number, ____**chemical symbol**____, and ____**average atomic mass**____ for the element.

Vertical columns in the table are called ____**groups (or families)**____. Most elements in a column have the same number of ____**electrons**____ in the outer energy level and tend to have similar ____**properties**____.

Horizontal rows in the table are called ____**periods**____. The elements on the left side of the table are ____**metals**____. Groups 3–12 contain metals known as ____**transition elements**____.

Elements on the right side are ____**nonmetals.**____

Chapter 11

REINFORCEMENT

Use with Text Pages 304–311

Kinds of Chemical Bonds

Answer the questions about the diagram shown below. Write your answers in the spaces provided.

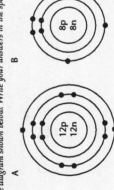

A (12p 12n)   B (8p 8n)

1. How many electrons will atom A lose to atom B? **2**

2. What kind of chemical bond will be formed between atom A and atom B if atom A loses electrons and atom B gains these electrons? **an ionic bond**

3. If atom A gives up electrons to atom B, what will the electrical charge of atom A be? **2+**

4. If atom B gains electrons from atom A, what will the electrical charge of atom B be? Why? **2−; Atom B will have two more electrons than it has protons. This will result in the entire atom having a negative charge.**

5. What is an atom with an electrical charge called? **an ion**

6. If atom A and atom B form a compound, what will the total charge of the compound be? Why? **The compound will be neutral because the positive charges of atom A will be equal to the negative charges of atom B.**

Complete the table comparing ionic compounds and covalent compounds.

Characteristic	Ionic	Covalent
How formed	**Atoms gain or lose electrons to other atoms.**	Electrons are shared by atoms.
Smallest particles	**ions**	molecules
Usual state of compound at room temperature	**solid**	liquid or gas

47

Chapter 11

REINFORCEMENT

Use with Text Pages 312–313

Hazardous Compounds at Home

Classify each of the hazardous materials listed in the table below as toxic, corrosive, or flammable. Place a check mark (✔) in the correct column of the table. More than one column may be checked.

Product	Toxic	Corrosive	Flammable
Insect spray	✔		
Gasoline	✔		✔
Paint thinner	✔		✔
Battery acid	✔	✔	
Bleach	✔	✔	
Antifreeze	✔		
Drain cleaner	✔	✔	
Oven cleaner	✔	✔	
Kerosene	✔		✔
Toilet cleaner	✔	✔	
Disinfectants	✔		

Answer the following questions on the lines provided.

1. How is a corrosive material harmful to the human body? **A corrosive material attacks and destroys the tissues that make up the human body.**

2. How can hazardous materials that get into the groundwater supply be harmful to humans? **The hazardous materials that enter the groundwater can pass unchanged through sewage treatment plants and enter the supply of drinking water.**

3. What kinds of products can be used in place of aerosols? **gels, lotions, nonaerosol sprays**

4. How would you share your knowledge of hazardous household chemicals with others? **Accept all reasonable answers.**

5. What is a safe alternative to using drain cleaner to unplug a clogged drain? **a plumber's snake or a plunger**

6. What does *toxic* mean? **poisonous**

7. Why should household cleaning products be stored in a place where children and animals cannot easily get them? **Many household products contain hazardous materials that could be dangerous for children or pets.**

8. What should you do with the oil you remove from a car during an oil change? **Recycle it.**

48

Chapter 11
REINFORCEMENT

Formulas and Names of Compounds

Use the Periodic Table of Elements on pages 286–287 of your textbook to identify the oxidation numbers of the elements in each group.

1+   1. any element in Group 1   0   4. any element in Group 18

1–   2. any element in Group 17   2–   5. any element in Group 16

2+   3. any element in Group 2

Answer the following questions in the spaces provided. Use the periodic table if you need help.

1. What is the usual oxidation number of oxygen?   2–

2. What is the usual oxidation number of hydrogen?   1+

3. What name is given to many of the elements that have more than one oxidation number?   **transition elements**

4. What is the sum of the oxidation numbers in a compound?   **zero**

5. What is an oxidation number? **a positive or negative number assigned to an element to show its combining ability in a compound**

Write the formulas for the following compounds. Use the Periodic Table of the Elements in your textbook for help.

1. copper(II) sulfate   **CuSO₄**
2. calcium chloride   **CaCl₂**
3. iron(II) oxide   **FeO**
4. copper(I) oxide   **Cu₂O**
5. sodium sulfide   **Na₂S**

Complete the following table by providing the name of the compound and the total number of atoms in each formula given.

Formula	Name	Number of atoms
NH₄OH	ammonium hydroxide	7
NH₄Cl	ammonium chloride	6
Ag₂O	silver oxide	3
K₂SO₄	potassium sulfate	7
Ca(NO₃)₂	calcium nitrate	9
Na₂S	sodium sulfide	3

Chapter 12
REINFORCEMENT

Metals

Complete the table below by writing the name of each of the following metals under the correct heading. Use the periodic table on pages 286–287 of your textbook if you need help.

beryllium   cadmium   calcium   cesium
strontium   cobalt   copper   francium
gold   lithium   magnesium   mercury
potassium   iron   nickel   silver
sodium   zinc   radium

Alkali metals	Alkaline earth metals	Transition elements	
sodium	calcium	iron	gold
francium	beryllium	copper	zinc
potassium	strontium	silver	mercury
cesium	magnesium	cobalt	nickel
lithium	radium	cadmium	

Write the letter of the term or phrase that best completes each statement.

b   1. The elements that make up the iron triad are _____.
   a. radioactive   c. alkali metals
   b. magnetic   d. alkaline earth metals

b   2. The alkaline earth metals make up _____ of the periodic table.
   a. group 1   b. group 2   c. group 17   d. group 18

a   3. The alkali metals make up _____ of the periodic table.
   a. group 1   b. group 2   c. group 16   d. group 18

c   4. The transition elements are in groups _____.
   a. 1–12   b. 3–13   c. 3–12   d. 3–5

b   5. Typical transition elements are metals that have _____ electrons in their outer energy levels.
   a. one   b. one or two   c. three   d. three or four

d   6. The most highly reactive of all metals are the _____.
   a. coinage metals   c. iron triad
   b. alkaline earth metals   d. alkali metals

Chapter 12
REINFORCEMENT

New Elements, New Properties

Use the periodic table on pages 286–287 of your textbook to answer questions 1–8.

1. What is the name of the group of elements with atomic numbers of 58–71? **lanthanoid series**

2. What is the name of the group of elements with atomic numbers 90–103? **actinoid series**

3. In what period do the elements in the actinide series belong? **period 7**

4. In what period do the elements in the lanthanide series belong? **period 6**

5. How many elements make up the lanthanide series? **14**

6. a. Which element in the lanthanide series has the highest atomic number? **lutetium**

   b. What is the atomic mass of this element? **174.967**

7. a. Which element in the actinide series has the greatest atomic number? **lawrencium**

   b. How many protons are in the nucleus of one atom of this element? **103**

8. List the names of the elements that make up the lanthanide series in order from greatest atomic mass to least atomic mass. **lutetium, ytterbium, thulium, erbium, holmium, dysprosium, terbium, gadolinium, europium, samarium, promethium, neodymium, praseodymium, cerium**

9. How does the lanthanide series compare to the actinide series? **They both include elements that have similar electron structures and similar properties.**

10. What is one practical use of the element americium? **This element is used in smoke detectors.**

11. Which elements in the actinide series are transuranium elements? **neptunium, plutonium, americium, curium, berkelium, californium, einsteinium, fermium, mendelevium, nobelium, and lawrencium**

Chapter 12
REINFORCEMENT

Nonmetals

Complete the following table that compares the properties of metals and nonmetals by supplying the information requested.

Characteristic	Metal	Nonmetal
Appearance of solid	shiny	dull
Is it malleable?	yes	no
Is it ductile?	yes	no
Does it conduct heat well?	yes	no
Does it conduct electricity well?	yes	no
Most common state at room temperature	solid	gas
Type(s) of bonding	metallic and ionic	ionic and covalent

In the spaces provided, list two properties for each nonmetal listed. **Answers may vary. Accept all correct responses.**

1. Hydrogen **gas, forms diatomic molecules, highly reactive**

2. Fluorine **active gas, forms diatomic molecules, 7 electrons in outer energy level**

3. Chlorine **gas, forms diatomic molecules, 7 electrons in outer energy level**

4. Bromine **liquid at room temperature, 7 electrons in outer energy level**

5. Iodine **shiny, gray solid, sublimates, 7 electrons in outer energy level**

6. Helium **2 electrons in outer energy level, not reactive, gas**

7. Neon **8 electrons in outer energy level, not reactive, gas**

Answer the following questions on the lines provided.

8. How does helium differ from the other noble gases? **Helium has two electrons in its outer energy level. The remaining noble gases each have eight electrons in their outer energy.**

9. How does bromine differ from the other nonmetals? **Bromine is the only nonmetal that is a liquid at room temperature.**

10. How does the location of hydrogen on the periodic table differ from the locations of the other nonmetals? **Hydrogen is the only nonmetal on the left side of the periodic table.**

Chapter 13

REINFORCEMENT • Simple Organic Compounds

Use the structural formulas below to answer the questions.

A.
```
      H
      |
  H - C - H
      |
      H
```

B.
```
      H   H   H
      |   |   |
  H - C - C = C - H
      |
      H
```

C.
```
      H   H   H   H
      |   |   |   |
  H - C - C - C - C - H
      |   |   |   |
      H   H   H   H
```

D.
```
      H   H   H
      |   |   |
  H - C - C - C - H
      |   |   |
      H   H   H
          |
      H - C - H
          |
          H
```

E.
```
      H
      |
  H - C - C ≡ C - H
      |
      H
```

1. What is the chemical formula for the compound shown in Figure A? __CH₄__

2. What is the chemical formula for Figure C? __C₄H₁₀__

3. Which compounds are unsaturated hydrocarbons? __B and E__

4. Which compounds are saturated hydrocarbons? __A, C, and D__

5. In Figure B, what is represented by the symbol = ? __a double bond__

6. In Figure E, what is represented by the symbol ≡ ? __a triple bond__

7. What is the chemical formula for Figure D? __C₄H₁₀__

8. Which two formulas represent isomers of the same compound? __C and D__

9. If the name of the substance in Figure C is butane, what is the name of the substance in

   Figure D? __isobutane__

10. What kind of organic compound is shown in all the formulas? __hydrocarbon__

Chapter 12

REINFORCEMENT • Mixed Groups

The elements that make up groups 13–16 of the periodic table are listed below. Classify each element as a metal, nonmetal, or metalloid by writing its name under the correct heading in the table. Use the periodic table of the elements on pages 286–287 of your textbook if you need help.

Boron Group
boron
aluminum
gallium
indium
thallium

Nitrogen Group
nitrogen
phosphorus
arsenic
antimony
bismuth

Carbon Group
carbon
silicon
germanium
tin
lead

Oxygen Group
oxygen
sulfur
selenium
tellurium
polonium

Metals	Nonmetals	Metalloids
aluminum	carbon	boron
gallium	nitrogen	silicon
indium	phosphorus	germanium
thallium	oxygen	antimony
tin	sulfur	tellurium
lead	selenium	polonium
bismuth		arsenic

Allotropes are different forms of the same element having different molecular structures. Diamond and graphite are allotropes of carbon. Look at the diagrams. Label each drawing as the structure for graphite or the structure for diamond.

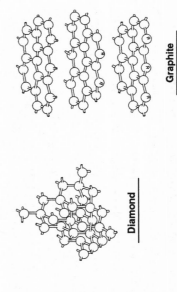

__Diamond__

__Graphite__

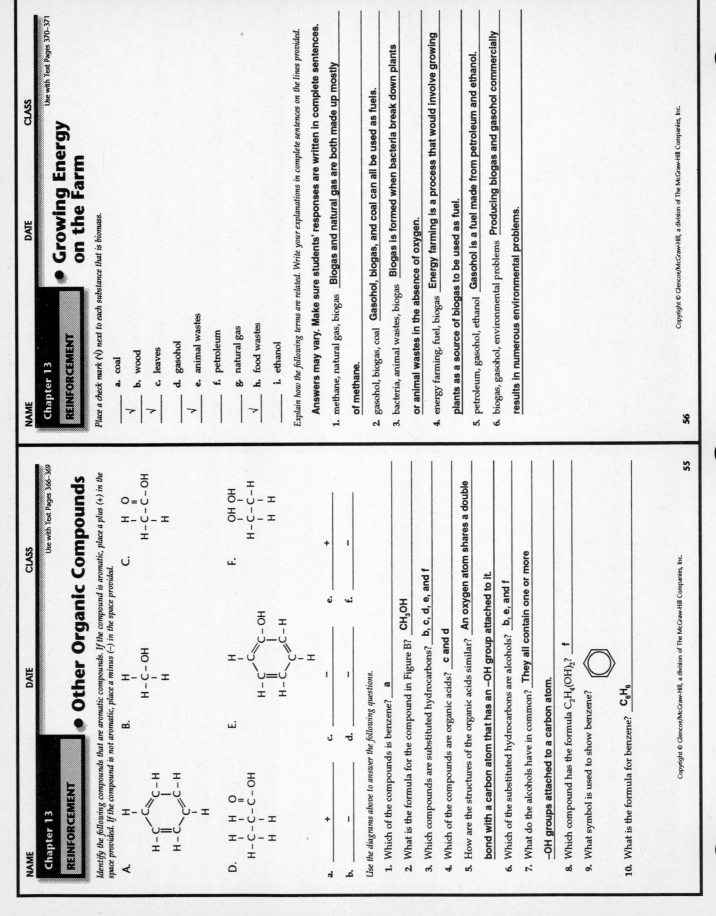

NAME _____ DATE _____ CLASS _____

Chapter 13
REINFORCEMENT

• Other Organic Compounds

Identify the following compounds that are aromatic compounds. If the compound is aromatic, place a plus (+) in the space provided. If the compound is not aromatic, place a minus (−) in the space provided.

A. [structure]   B. H–C–OH structure   C. [structure]

D. [structure]   E. [structure]   F. [structure]

a. +
b. −
c. −
d. −
e. +
f. −

Use the diagrams above to answer the following questions.

1. Which of the compounds is benzene? **a**
2. What is the formula for the compound in Figure B? **CH₃OH**
3. Which compounds are substituted hydrocarbons? **b, c, d, e, and f**
4. Which of the compounds are organic acids? **c and d**
5. How are the structures of the organic acids similar? **An oxygen atom shares a double bond with a carbon atom that has an –OH group attached to it.**
6. Which of the substituted hydrocarbons are alcohols? **b, e, and f**
7. What do the alcohols have in common? **They all contain one or more –OH groups attached to a carbon atom.**
8. Which compound has the formula $C_2H_4(OH)_2$? **f**
9. What symbol is used to show benzene? [hexagon]
10. What is the formula for benzene? **C_6H_6**

NAME _____ DATE _____ CLASS _____

Chapter 13
REINFORCEMENT

• Growing Energy on the Farm

Place a check mark (√) next to each substance that is biomass.

____ a. coal
√ b. wood
√ c. leaves
____ d. gasohol
√ e. animal wastes
____ f. petroleum
____ g. natural gas
√ h. food wastes
____ i. ethanol

Explain how the following terms are related. Write your explanations in complete sentences on the lines provided.

Answers may vary. Make sure students' responses are written in complete sentences.

1. methane, natural gas, biogas Biogas and natural gas are both made up mostly of methane.
2. gasohol, biogas, coal Gasohol, biogas, and coal can all be used as fuels.
3. bacteria, animal wastes, biogas Biogas is formed when bacteria break down plants or animal wastes in the absence of oxygen.
4. energy farming, fuel, biogas Energy farming is a process that would involve growing plants as a source of biogas to be used as fuel.
5. petroleum, gasohol, ethanol Gasohol is a fuel made from petroleum and ethanol.
6. biogas, gasohol, environmental problems Producing biogas and gasohol commercially results in numerous environmental problems.

Chapter 13

REINFORCEMENT

• Biological Compounds

Use with Text Pages 373–379

Complete the table below by placing a check mark (√) in the column of each kind of organic compound that has each characteristic.

Characteristic	Protein	Nucleic Acid	Carbohydrate	Lipid
1. enzymes are an example	√			
2. includes fats and oils				√
3. polymers formed from amino acids	√			
4. is a polymer	√	√	√	
5. always contains carbon and hydrogen	√	√	√	√
6. is made up of nucleotides		√		
7. includes DNA and RNA		√		
8. RNA controls the production of these	√			
9. includes sugar			√	
10. Its monomers contain –NH₂ and –COOH groups	√			
11. controls cell reproduction and activities		√		
12. ratio of hydrogen to oxygen is 2:1			√	
13. is held together with peptide bonds	√			
14. glucose is an example			√	
15. includes starches			√	
16. includes cholesterol				√
17. accounts for 15% of your weight	√			
18. made up of monomers	√	√	√	
19. molecule is ladder-shaped and twisted		√		
20. is an organic compound	√	√	√	√

Chapter 14

REINFORCEMENT

• Materials with a Past

Use with Text Pages 388–395

On the lines provided, write the letters of the substances in Column II that make up each alloy listed in Column I.

Column I	Column II
a, d 1. bronze	a. copper
a, c 2. brass	b. mercury
b, c, f 3. dental amalgam	c. zinc
e, i 4. aluminum-lithium	d. tin
g, h 5. steel	e. aluminum
	f. silver
	g. iron
	h. carbon
	i. lithium

Name one practical use for each alloy listed below. **Answers will vary. Suggested answers are given.**

6. brass **trophies, musical instruments**

7. steel **building materials, car parts**

8. bronze **statues, plumbing fixtures**

9. amalgam **dental fillings**

10. gold alloys **jewelry, decorative products**

Answer the following questions on the lines provided.

11. What is a ceramic? **a material made from dried clay or claylike mixtures**

12. What are structural ceramics? **ceramics such as bricks and tile that are used as building materials in the construction industry**

13. What two elements are often mixed with structural ceramics? **silicon and aluminum**

14. How does glass differ from other ceramics? **Glass does not have particles that are arranged in regular crystal patterns.**

15. What is the major ingredient in glass? **silicon dioxide, or sand**

16. What is a cermet? **a material made up of ceramics and metals that is designed to have some characteristics of both**

17. List three uses of ceramic products. **Answers may vary. Likely responses include bricks, floor and wall tiles, dishes, and pottery.**

18. How does adding pigment to glass affect the glass? **Pigments change the color of glass.**

Chapter 14
REINFORCEMENT

● Record Breaking with Sports Technology

Complete the following table by listing a new material being used for each type of equipment and one advantage that the equipment has compared with former equipment.

Equipment	New material	Advantage
speed skate blade	steel and carbon composite	reduces mass/reduces air drag
speed skate shoe	carbon composites	reduces mass/reduces air drag
speed skating suit	silicon-based polymers	direct wind current for a slight air pressure advantage
skis	plastics	stabilize skis during jumping
racing car body	carbon and boron fibers	reduces weight
tennis racket	carbon and boron composites	strength/speed
golf club	boron composites	more powerful swing

Answer the following questions in complete sentences.

1. Many improvements in sports performance have been brought about by using scientific analysis to change what areas of athletics? **Scientific analysis has led to changes in training methods, athlete nutrition, and coaching techniques.**

2. Cite one way in which sports technology might affect sports events and their records.
Answers will vary. New technologies in equipment may lead to improved speeds and therefore reduced record times of athletes in such areas as speed skating, running events, bobsledding, and auto racing. New technologies may lead to increased speed and power in equipment and therefore affect serving speed and accuracy in tennis, distances in golf, and number of home runs in baseball.

Chapter 14
REINFORCEMENT

● New Materials

Determine whether the italicized term makes each statement true or false. If the statement is true, write the word "true" in the blank. If the statement is false, write in the blank the term that makes the statement true.

polymer 1. A gigantic molecule made from thousands of smaller molecules is called a *monomer*.

polymer 2. Polyethylene is an example of a synthetic *monomer*.

true 3. Proteins are examples of natural *polymers*.

synthetic 4. Plastics are examples of *natural* polymers.

true 5. A material that is made artificially in the laboratory is called a *synthetic* material.

ethene molecules 6. The monomers that make up polyethylene are *nucleic acids*.

true 7. A *synthetic fiber* is a strand of a synthetic polymer.

true 8. An example of a synthetic fiber is *nylon*.

petroleum 9. Most of the raw materials that are used to make plastics come from *protein* products.

true 10. Plastic and synthetic fibers are sometimes called *petrochemical* products.

composite 11. Reinforced concrete is an example of a *plastic*.

glass 12. Fiberglass is a composite made up of plastic and *concrete*.

Answer the following questions on the lines provided.

13. What does the term *composite* mean? **made up of two or more parts**

14. What materials are used to make fiberglass? **plastic and glass**

15. How does the use of synthetic products such as plastic increase the use of fossil fuels?
Plastics are made from petroleum products, so increased use of plastics increases the amounts of fossil fuels used.

Chapter 15

REINFORCEMENT

● How Solutions Form

Complete the table below by writing the missing information in the appropriate box. Then answer the following questions. **Student examples may vary. Accept all logical examples.**

Solution Type	Solvent	Solute	Example
gas	**gas**	gas	air
liquid	**liquid**	solid	salt water
solid	**solid**	liquid	dental amalgam
liquid	liquid	**gas**	club soda
liquid	liquid	**liquid**	vinegar
solid	solid	**solid**	brass

Study the information in your table carefully. What is true about the state of the solvent and the type of solution produced? **The state of the solvent is the same as the state of the solution.**

Circle the term in parentheses that makes each statement true.

1. A solid dissolves faster in a liquid if the temperature of the liquid is ((increased) decreased).

2. A gas dissolves faster in a liquid if the temperature of the liquid is (increased (decreased)).

3. The ((larger) smaller) the surface area of a solid, the faster it will dissolve.

4. When a gas is being dissolved in a liquid, stirring (speeds up (slows down)) the dissolving process.

5. When a solid is being dissolved in a liquid, stirring ((speeds up) slows down) the dissolving process.

6. A gas dissolves faster in a liquid when under ((high) low) pressure.

Study your responses to the exercise above. Use your responses to answer the following question.

7. How do the methods of speeding the rate of solution for dissolving a solid in a liquid compare to the methods of speeding the rate of solution when dissolving a gas in a liquid? **Heating the liquid solvent and stirring speed up the dissolving rate of a solid solute and slow the dissolving rate of a gas solute. Pressure has no effect on a solid solute. Increasing surface area is not applicable to a gas solute.**

Chapter 15

REINFORCEMENT

● Regulating Organic Solvents

Write your answers to the following questions and activities in the spaces provided.

1. Why may the buildings in which people live be hazardous to their health? **Scientists have warned that a number of potentially harmful chemicals are found in materials currently used in construction and remodeling.**

2. What are some examples of construction and remodeling materials that contain organic solvents? **glues, paints, paint removers, paint and varnish thinners, some caulking compounds, and carpeting**

3. What physical property of organic solvents makes them useful and also makes them potentially hazardous? **Organic solvents vaporize easily.**

4. In what two ways can organic solvents enter the body? **Organic solvents can enter the body by being absorbed through the skin or their fumes can be inhaled.**

5. What are some harmful effects of many organic solvents? **Many organic solvents are substances that are known to affect the nervous system and cause growth and development problems. In some instances, a few have been shown to cause cancer.**

6. What regulations has the United States Occupational Safety and Heath Administration (OSHA) established for workers who come into contact with organic solvents? **OSHA establishes time limits beyond which a worker cannot be exposed to health-threatening solvents.**

7. What regulations has the Consumer Product Safety Commission (CPSC) established about materials potentially harmful to health? **CPSC requires labels on all corrosive or flammable chemicals. Some labels list harmful ingredients and itemize the dangers to health.**

8. How does OSHA penalize companies that violate regulations protecting employees? **Fines may be incurred if workers are found to be exposed to solvents for extended periods of time.**

9. Why is good ventilation an important requirement when working with harmful fumes or organic solvents? **Moving air removes the potentially harmful fumes of organic solvents so that they are not inhaled.**

Left worksheet:

REINFORCEMENT

Solubility and Concentration

Use with Text Pages 424–431

Use the information in the table to graph the solubility curves for barium hydroxide, Ba(OH)₂; copper(II) sulfate,
CuSO₄; potassium chloride, KCl; and sodium nitrate, NaNO₃. Use a different colored pencil for each compound.

Solubility in g/100 g water

Compound	Temperature			
	0°C	20°C	60°C	100°C
$Ba(OH)_2$	1.67	3.89	20.94	101.40
$CuSO_4$	23.10	32.00	61.80	114.00
KCl	28.0	34.2	45.8	56.30
$NaNO_3$	73.0	87.6	122.0	180.00

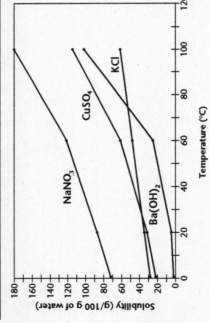

Use the information in the table and your graph to answer the following questions.

1. At about what temperature will 100 g of water dissolve equal amounts of potassium chloride
and barium hydroxide? __about 73°C__

2. At about what temperature will 37 g of both copper(II) sulfate and potassium chloride dissolve
in 100 g of water? __about 27°C__

3. If 100 g of sodium nitrate are dissolved in 100 g of water at 60°C, is the solution formed
saturated, unsaturated, or supersaturated? __unsaturated__

4. If 32 g of copper(II) sulfate are dissolved in 100 g of water at 20°C, is the solution produced
saturated, unsaturated, or supersaturated? __saturated__

63

Right worksheet:

REINFORCEMENT

Particles in Solution

Use with Text Pages 432–434

Use the diagram below to answer questions 1–10.

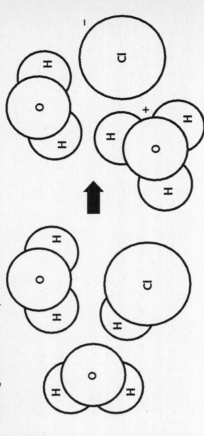

1. Is water a polar molecule or a nonpolar molecule? How do you know? __polar; one end of__
__the water molecule pulls the H⁺ from HCl__

2. Is HCl polar or nonpolar? __polar__

3. What is the general rule that determines how polar and nonpolar substances dissolve?
__Like dissolves like.__

4. Will HCl dissolve in water? __yes__

5. What happens to the HCl molecule when it is placed in water? __The force of attraction__
__between the opposite charges of the molecules separates the molecules of the polar__
__solute and the solute ionizes.__

6. What happens to the hydrogen atom of the HCl molecule? __It is attracted to the negative__
__end of the water molecule.__

7. What happens to the chlorine atom of the HCl molecule? __It becomes a chloride ion, Cl⁻.__

8. What is the process shown in the diagram called? __ionization__

9. Is HCl an electrolyte or a nonelectrolyte? __an electrolyte__

10. Will the solution conduct electricity? __yes__

64

Chapter 16

REINFORCEMENT

● Chemical Reactions—Up in the Air

Use the information in Section 16-2 to write the following equations and answer the questions.

1. Write a word equation that explains how chlorine reacts with ozone. **Chlorine gas plus ozone gas produces chlorine monoxide gas plus oxygen gas.**

2. Write a chemical equation for the word equation you wrote in number 1. Be sure to indicate the state of each substance involved in the reaction. **$Cl(g) + O_3(g) \rightarrow ClO(g) + O_2(g)$**

3. What are the reactants in this chemical equation? **chlorine and ozone**

4. What are the products? **chlorine monoxide and oxygen**

5. What allotrope of oxygen has the formula O_3? **ozone**

Answer the following questions with complete sentences in the spaces provided.

6. How do CFCs harm the environment? **Chlorine in the CFCs breaks down the ozone in the atmosphere.**

7. Why is the ozone layer important to living things? **The ozone layer protects living things from harmful ultraviolet rays given off by the sun.**

8. What are CFCs? **CFCs are compounds called chlorofluorocarbons made up of chlorine, fluorine, and carbon.**

9. How are CFCs useful? **CFCs are used in coolants such as those used in refrigerators and air conditioners.**

10. The number of cases of skin cancer increases as the protection against UV rays from the sun provided by the ozone layer decreases. What can you infer about the cause of skin cancer? **Ultraviolet rays from the sun are a cause of skin cancer.**

Student responses may vary somewhat. Check students' answers to be sure that they're written in complete sentences.

Chapter 16

REINFORCEMENT

● Chemical Changes in Matter

Use the equations to answer the questions.

$Zn(cr) + S(cr) \rightarrow ZnS(cr)$

1. What are the reactants in this chemical reaction? **zinc and sulfur**

2. What is the product? **zinc sulfide**

3. What is the state of both the reactants and the products? **All are solids.**

4. According to the law of conservation of mass, if the total mass of the product in this chemical reaction is 14 grams, what must the combined masses of the reactants be? **14 grams**

$2H_2(g) + O_2(g) \rightarrow 2H_2O(l)$

5. What is the product in this reaction? **H_2O, or water**

6. What are the reactants? **hydrogen and oxygen**

7. What are the states of the reactants in this reaction? **Both are gases.**

8. What is the state of the product? **liquid**

9. What do the coefficients tell you about the ratio of the reactants? **It takes twice as many units of hydrogen as it does units of oxygen in the reaction.**

10. How many units of the product are produced? **2**

Write chemical equations for the following reactions.

11. Two units of solid sodium plus one unit of chlorine gas produce two units of sodium chloride, a solid. **$2Na(cr) + Cl_2(g) \rightarrow 2NaCl(cr)$**

12. One unit of methane gas, CH_4, plus two units of oxygen gas produce one unit of carbon dioxide gas, CO_2, and two units of liquid water. **$CH_4(g) + 2O_2(g) \rightarrow CO_2(g) + 2H_2O(l)$**

13. One unit of aqueous aluminum sulfate plus three units of aqueous barium chloride yield two units of aqueous aluminum chloride plus three units of solid barium sulfate. **$Al_2(SO_4)_3(aq) + 3BaCl_2(aq) \rightarrow 2AlCl_3(aq) + 3BaSO_4(cr)$**

Chapter 16

REINFORCEMENT

Chemical Equations

Answer the following questions with complete sentences.

1. What is a balanced chemical equation? <u>A balanced chemical equation has the same</u>

<u>number of atoms of each element on both sides of the equation.</u>

2. Use the law of conservation of mass to explain why a chemical equation must be balanced. <u>According to the law of conservation of mass, matter cannot be created or destroyed.</u> <u>Therefore, in a chemical reaction, the sum of the masses of the reactants must equal</u> <u>the sum of the masses of the products.</u>

Balance the following equations. If you need help, review the steps for balancing equations on page 449 of your textbook.

3. $H_2(g) + O_2(g) \rightarrow H_2O(l)$
$2H_2(g) + O_2(g) \rightarrow 2H_2O(l)$

4. $N_2(g) + H_2(g) \rightarrow NH_3(g)$
$N_2(g) + 3H_2(g) \rightarrow 2NH_3(g)$

5. $Li(cr) + FeBr_2(aq) \rightarrow LiBr(aq) + Fe(cr)$
$2Li(cr) + FeBr_2(aq) \rightarrow 2LiBr(aq) + Fe(cr)$

6. $Al(cr) + HCl(aq) \rightarrow AlCl_3(aq) + H_2(g)$
$2Al(cr) + 6HCl(aq) \rightarrow 2AlCl_3(aq) + 3H_2(g)$

7. $Li(cr) + N_2(g) \rightarrow Li_3N(cr)$
$6Li(cr) + N_2(g) \rightarrow 2Li_3N(cr)$

Chapter 16

REINFORCEMENT

Types of Chemical Reactions

Match each type of chemical reaction in Column II with its description in Column I. Write the letter of the correct reaction in the space provided.

Column I

d 1. A precipitate, water, or a gas forms when two ionic compounds are dissolved in a solution.

a 2. Two or more substances combine to form another substance.

c 3. One element replaces another in a compound.

b 4. A substance breaks down into two or more simpler substances.

Column II

a. synthesis reaction
b. decomposition reaction
c. single displacement reaction
d. double displacement reaction

Classify each of the following chemical reactions as a synthesis reaction, decomposition reaction, single displacement reaction, or double displacement reaction. Write the name of the reaction type on the line on the right.

5. $4Fe(cr) + 3O_2(g) \rightarrow 2Fe_2O_3(cr)$ <u>synthesis reaction</u>

6. $Zn(cr) + 2HCl(aq) \rightarrow ZnCl_2(aq) + H_2(g)$ <u>single displacement reaction</u>

7. $MgCO_3(aq) + 2HCl(aq) \rightarrow MgCl_2(aq) + H_2O(l) + CO_2(g)$ <u>double displacement reaction</u>

8. $NiCl_2(cr) \rightarrow Ni(cr) + Cl_2(g)$ <u>decomposition reaction</u>

9. $4C(cr) + 6H_2(g) + O_2(g) \rightarrow 2C_2H_6O(cr)$ <u>synthesis reaction</u>

10. $C_{12}H_{22}O_{11}(cr) \rightarrow 12C(cr) + 11H_2O(g)$ <u>decomposition reaction</u>

11. $2LiI(aq) + Pb(NO_3)_2(aq) \rightarrow 2LiNO_3(aq) + PbI_2(cr)$ <u>double displacement reaction</u>

12. $CdCO_3(cr) \rightarrow CdO(cr) + CO_2(g)$ <u>decomposition reaction</u>

13. $Cl_2(g) + 2KBr(aq) \rightarrow 2KCl(aq) + Br_2(g)$ <u>single displacement reaction</u>

14. $BaCl_2(aq) + 2KIO_3(aq) \rightarrow Ba(IO_3)_2(cr) + 2KCl(aq)$ <u>double displacement reaction</u>

Chapter 16

REINFORCEMENT

Energy and Chemical Reactions

Answer the following questions with complete sentences.

1. What is a catalyst? A catalyst is a chemical substance that speeds up a chemical reaction without undergoing a permanent change itself.

2. What is an exothermic reaction? An exothermic reaction is a reaction that gives off more energy than it requires.

3. What is an inhibitor? An inhibitor is any substance that slows down a reaction.

4. What is an endothermic reaction? An endothermic reaction requires energy for the reaction to take place.

Identify whether each reaction described involves a catalyst, an inhibitor, or neither. Write C for catalyst, I for inhibitor, or N for neither in the space at the left.

__N__ 5. Placing oil on a metal part helps to keep the part from rusting. Is the oil a catalyst, an inhibitor, or neither?

__C__ 6. In the human body, proteins called enzymes help to speed up chemical processes. The proteins are not changed during these chemical processes. Are the enzymes catalysts, inhibitors, or neither?

__N__ 7. Painting a metal surface keeps water from touching the metal and causing the metal to rust. Is the paint a catalyst, an inhibitor, or neither?

__I__ 8. Food preservatives called BHT and BHA slow down the spoilage of certain foods. Are BHT and BHA catalysts, inhibitors, or neither?

__C__ 9. Nickel is used to increase the rate of methane formation from the addition of hydrogen and carbon monoxide. Nickel does not permanently change. Is nickel a catalyst, inhibitor, or neither?

Identify whether each reaction described below is endothermic or exothermic. In the blank, write EN for endothermic or EX for exothermic.

__EX__ 10. When a lit match is placed in alcohol, the alcohol ignites producing heat and light.

__EN__ 11. Energy in the form of electricity can be added to water to break apart the water molecules into hydrogen gas and oxygen gas.

__EX__ 12. A piece of coal placed in a furnace gives off heat and light before turning to ash.

__EN__ 13. When ammonium chloride mixes with water, the solution formed feels cold.

Chapter 17

REINFORCEMENT

Acids and Bases

Identify each item listed below as to whether it refers to an acid, a base, or both an acid and a base. Use the letters in the key.

KEY: A = acid   B = base   AB = acid and base

__A__ 1. sour taste
__B__ 2. bitter taste
__A__ 3. produces hydrogen ions in solution
__AB__ 4. is an electrolyte
__B__ 5. is slippery
__AB__ 6. is often corrosive
__B__ 7. exists as a crystalline solid in an undissolved state
__B__ 8. produces hydroxide ions in solution
__AB__ 9. can be detected with an indicator
__B__ 10. Soaps are an example.
__AB__ 11. may be used to make fertilizer
__A__ 12. is used in pickling
__A__ 13. forms through ionization
__B__ 14. forms through dissociation
__A__ 15. Compounds that produce this in solution are made up of polar molecules.
__A__ 16. produces hydronium ions
__B__ 17. Most compounds that produce this in aqueous solution are ionic.
__AB__ 18. exists in aqueous solution
__A__ 19. HCl is an example.
__B__ 20. Ammonia is a common example.
__AB__ 21. conducts electricity

Complete the following. Write your answers on the lines provided.

22. Use the information above to identify four properties that acids and bases have in common. Acids and bases exist only in aqueous solution, are electrolytes, are often corrosive, and can be detected with an indicator.

23. Identify three characteristics of acids that are NOT true of bases. Acids have a sour taste, produce hydrogen ions in solution, and are formed through ionization of compounds that have polar molecules.

24. Identify three characteristics of bases that acids do NOT have. Bases have a bitter taste and feel slippery, produce hydroxide ions in solution, and form through dissociation of ionic compounds in solution.

_____

_____

Chapter 17

REINFORCEMENT

• Strength of Acids and Bases

Use with Text Pages 474–477

The pH values of several common substances are listed below. Place each item from the list on the pH scale in its proper location. The first one has been done for you.

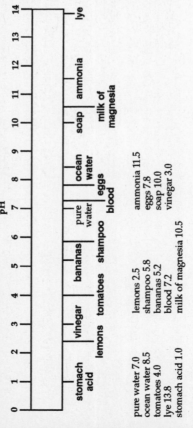

pH scale (0 to 14):

- stomach acid
- lemons
- vinegar
- tomatoes
- bananas
- shampoo
- pure water
- blood
- eggs
- ocean water
- soap
- ammonia
- milk of magnesia
- lye

pure water 7.0
ocean water 8.5
tomatoes 4.0
lye 13.8
stomach acid 1.0

lemons 2.5
shampoo 5.8
bananas 5.2
blood 7.2
milk of magnesia 10.5

ammonia 11.5
eggs 7.8
soap 10.0
vinegar 3.0

Complete the table below by writing the name of each of the substances above under the proper heading. Place substances with a pH lower than 3.0 in the strong acids column. Place substances with a pH higher than 10.0 in the strong bases column.

Strong acids	Weak acids	Weak bases	Strong bases
lemons	vinegar	soap	ammonia
stomach acid	shampoo	blood	lye
	tomatoes	ocean water	milk of magnesia
	bananas	eggs	

Answer the following questions on the lines provided.

1. Is pure water an acidic, basic, or neutral substance? neutral

2. How does the pH of a strong acid compare with the pH of a weak acid? The pH of a strong acid is lower than the pH of a weak acid.

3. How does the pH of a strong base compare with the pH of a weak base? The pH of a strong base is higher than the pH of a weak base.

4. How does the pH of an acid compare to the pH of a base? The pH of an acid is less than 7; the pH of a base is greater than 7.

Chapter 17

REINFORCEMENT

• Acid Rain

Use with Text Pages 478–479

Determine whether the italicized term makes each statement true or false. If the statement is true, write the word "true" in the blank. If the statement is false, write in the blank the term that makes the statement true.

__5.6__ 1. Normal rain has a pH of 7.0.

__true__ 2. Acid rain is ten times more acidic than normal rain.

__lower__ 3. Any form of precipitation with a pH higher than 5.6 is called acid rain.

__oxides__ 4. Scientists think that acid rain forms when carbonates of sulfur and nitrogen mix with rainwater.

__true__ 5. Sulfur and nitrogen oxides are released when nuclear fuel is burned.

__strong__ 6. Chemical washers on smoke stacks can reduce the amount of damaging gases released.

__true__ 7. Tiny aquatic plants and animals called plankton form the base of the food chain for small fish.

__true__ 8. When plankton die because of acid rain, the fish that depend upon them for food also die.

__dissolves__ 9. Acid rain melts important mineral nutrients that are found in soil.

__marble__ 10. Statues made of limestone and glass weather rapidly due to acid rain.

__true__ 11. Plants deprived of nutrients because of acid rain do NOT grow at a normal rate.

__are__ 12. Acid rain causes the most problems in countries that are not industrialized.

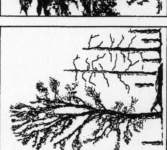

REINFORCEMENT

● Acid, Bases, and Salts

Use the equation below to answer questions 1–6.

$$HCl(aq) + NaOH(aq) \rightarrow H_2O(l) + NaCl(cr)$$

1. What type of reaction is shown?   **neutralization**

2. What are the products in this reaction?   **water (H_2O) and sodium chloride (NaCl)**

3. What are the reactants?   **HCl (an acid) and NaOH (a base)**

4. a. Which of the reactants shown is a base?   **NaOH**

   b. How do you know?   **It has an OH⁻ ion in its formula.**

5. a. Which of the reactants is an acid?   **HCl**

   b. What is the name of the acid?   **hydrochloric acid**

   c. Is the acid a strong acid or a weak acid?   **a strong acid**

6. What kind of compound is NaCl?   **a salt**

Identify the type of substance that is most likely to be formed by each reaction described below. Use the terms soap, salt, and ester.

   salt   7. hydrochloric acid and a base

   ester   8. an organic acid and an alcohol

   soap   9. sodium hydroxide and a fat

   ester   10. acetic acid and methyl alcohol

   soap   11. potassium hydroxide and oil

   salt   12. an acid and ammonia

Answer the following questions on the lines provided.

13. How does a soap made from sodium hydroxide differ from a soap made from potassium hydroxide?   **A soap made from sodium hydroxide is a solid. A soap made from potassium hydroxide is a liquid.**

14. Why are most laundry products detergents instead of soaps?   **Detergents do not react with hard water to form precipitates the way soaps do.**

15. What is an observable characteristic of an ester?   **Most esters have an odor.**

REINFORCEMENT

● Characteristics of Waves

On each of the figures below, 1 square of the grid represents 1 unit. Use Figure 1 to answer questions 1–4. On the blank, write the letter of the correct answer.

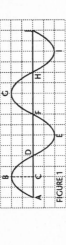

FIGURE 1

   d   1. Which distance is exactly 1 wavelength?

     a. A–J   b. A–D   c. D–F   d. B–G   e. D–J

   a   2. Which distance is the amplitude?

     a. B–C   b. A–D   c. E–G   d. E–I   e. A–J

   d   3. How many units measure one wavelength?

     a. 2   b. 4   c. 6   d. 8   e. 10

   d   4. Which letters are the crests?

     a. A, D   b. E, I   c. H, J   d. B, G   e. F, H

5. The wave in Figure 2 is identical to the wave in Figure 1. Use a red pencil to draw a wave between points A and B that has a wavelength of 4 units and an amplitude of 2 units.

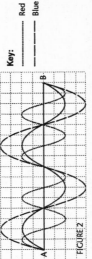

Key:
Red ———
Blue - - - -

FIGURE 2

6. Use a blue pencil to draw a second wave that has a wavelength of 8 units and an amplitude of 4 units.

7. Between points X and Y on Figure 3 draw a wave that has a wavelength of 4 units and an amplitude of 5 units.

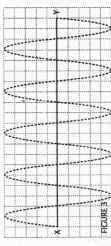

FIGURE 3

Chapter 18

REINFORCEMENT

Using Sound Advice in Medicine

Write your answers to the following questions and activities in the spaces provided.

1. What is ultrasonic technology? __Ultrasonic technology uses sounds with frequencies greater than 20 000 Hz to perform tasks.__

2. How do jewelers use ultrasonic sound? __Ultrasonic technology is used by jewelers to remove stubborn deposits from jewelry.__

3. How do chemists use ultrasonic technology? __Ultrasonic technology is used by chemists to clean glassware in ultrasonic baths.__

4. What is probably the best-known use of ultrasound in medicine? __monitoring the development of a fetus in a woman's uterus__

5. Physicians commonly use ultrasound to examine what abdominal organs? __liver, pancreas, gallbladder, and spleen__

6. How is the ultrasound Doppler shift used in medicine? __The ultrasound Doppler shift is used to gather information about bloodflow in cardiac patients.__

7. What are kidney stones? __hard deposits of calcium oxalate that form in the kidney__

8. How has ultrasound replaced surgery as a means of removing some kidney stones? __Instead of removing kidney stones surgically, ultrasound waves are used to create vibrations that can often break up the stones, after which the smaller pieces pass naturally from the body in the urine.__

Sequence from 1–5 the following steps in producing a sonogram, by writing the correct number of the step in the blank to the left of each statement.

__5__ Computer program converts electrical signals into video images.

__1__ Probe sends out high-frequency sound waves.

__4__ Sound waves produce electrical signals.

__3__ Sound waves reflect from organs and tissues.

__2__ Sound waves strike organs and tissues.

Chapter 18

REINFORCEMENT

The Nature of Sound

Determine whether the italicized term makes each statement true or false. If the statement is true, write the word "true" in the blank. If the statement is false, write in the blank the term that makes the statement true.

__true__ 1. A *rarefaction* is the area of a sound wave where particles are less dense.

__true__ 2. Sound travels more slowly through *gases* than it does through liquids.

__pitch__ 3. The *amplitude* of a sound is its highness or lowness.

__true__ 4. As the amplitude of a wave decreases, its *intensity* also increases.

__pitch or wave frequency__ 5. The Doppler effect is an apparent change in the *resonance* of a sound.

__true__ 6. As energy is added to a wave, its amplitude and *intensity* increase.

__true__ 7. The speed of a sound wave depends partly on the *temperature* of the medium.

__true__ 8. The pitch of a sound depends on the *frequency* of the waves that produce it.

__true__ 9. Air and water are examples of *media* through which sound travels.

__frequency, pitch__ 10. A high musical note has a higher *wavelength* than a low note.

__compressional__ 11. In a *transverse* wave, matter vibrates in the direction the wave travels.

In the drawing below, the freight train and the sports car are traveling beside each other at the same speed and the train whistle is blowing.

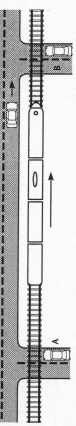

12. Compare the frequency of the sound waves produced by the whistle and the pitch of each of the following:

a. Michael, who is waiting to cross the tracks at point A __The frequency would decrease and the pitch would be lower.__

b. Sandra, who is driving the sports car __The frequency and the pitch would be the same.__

c. Tony, who is an engineer on the train __The frequency and the pitch would be the same.__

d. Jane, whose car has stopped at position B __The frequency would increase and the pitch would be higher.__

Chapter 19
REINFORCEMENT

Use with Text Pages 528–535

Electromagnetic Radiation

Radio waves	Microwaves	Infrared	Ultraviolet	X rays	Gamma rays
	Long/Short				

Optical →

← Increasing frequency →

Use the diagram to answer questions 1–9.

c   1. The wavelength of an electromagnetic wave is _____.
     a. directly proportional to its frequency   c. inversely proportional to its frequency
     b. inversely proportional to its velocity   d. none of the above

b   2. In a vacuum, all electromagnetic waves have _____.
     a. the same frequency   c. the same wavelength
     b. the same velocity   d. all of the above

a   3. All electromagnetic radiation in the optical portion of the electromagnetic spectrum _____.
     a. is visible   c. has the same frequency
     b. has the same wavelength   d. all the above

b   4. Compared to the photons of violet light, the photons of red light _____.
     a. have more energy   c. have equal energy
     b. have less energy   d. none of the above

d   5. Compared to radio waves, microwaves have _____.
     a. shorter wavelengths   c. higher frequencies
     b. photons with more energy   d. all of the above

a   6. Compared to gamma rays, X rays have _____.
     a. longer wavelengths   c. photons with more energy
     b. higher frequencies   d. all of the above

c   7. We perceive infrared waves as _____.
     a. coldness   c. warmth
     b. light   d. none of the above

c   8. Compared to gamma rays, radio waves have _____.
     a. shorter wavelengths   c. photons with less energy
     b. higher frequencies   d. none of the above

c   9. All objects emit _____.
     a. gamma rays   c. electromagnetic waves
     b. light   d. none of the above

Chapter 18
REINFORCEMENT

Use with Text Pages 516–521

Music to Your Ears

Combine the word parts below to form the answers to the clues below. Work carefully. A space has been left between each word part to help you. Place one letter on each blank, and be sure the number of letters in each word part matches the number of blanks. Cross out each word part as you use it. The first definition has been started for you to use as an example.

a	con	fer	mu	qua	struc	tive	ver
a	cous	fun	noise	re	tal	tive	ver
ance	da	~~in~~	o	res	tave	tion	
beats	de	li	oc	sic	~~ter~~	tones	
ber	ence	men	on	struc	tics	ty	

1. the ability of two or more waves to combine
 <u>I N</u>   <u>T E R</u>   <u>F E R</u>   <u>E N C E</u>

2. effect produced when a musical instrument vibrates
 <u>R E S</u>   <u>O N</u>   <u>A N C E</u>

3. variations of sound intensity
 <u>B E A T S</u>

4. type of interference that results in two waves canceling each other
 <u>D E</u>   <u>S T R U C</u>   <u>T I V E</u>

5. sound that has no set pattern or definite pitch
 <u>N O I S E</u>

6. describes the difference between two sounds having the same pitch
 <u>Q U A</u>   <u>L I</u>   <u>T Y</u>

7. the study of sound
 <u>A</u>   <u>C O U S</u>   <u>T I C S</u>

8. tone produced when an entire string vibrates up and down
 <u>F U N</u>   <u>D A</u>   <u>M E N</u>   <u>T A L</u>

9. sounds with specific pitches and qualities that follow a regular pattern
 <u>M U</u>   <u>S I C</u>

10. frequency range of the musical scale
 <u>O C</u>   <u>T A V E</u>

11. the type of interference that occurs when two wave crests arrive together
 <u>C O N</u>   <u>S T R U C</u>   <u>T I V E</u>

12. produced by vibrations that are multiples of the fundamental frequency
 <u>O</u>   <u>V E R</u>   <u>T O N E S</u>

13. the effect produced by many reflections of sounds
 <u>R E</u>   <u>V E R</u>   <u>B E R</u>   <u>A</u>   <u>T I O N</u>

Chapter 19
REINFORCEMENT

● Light and Color

Solve the following crossword puzzle by using the clues provided.

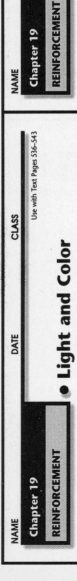

Across

3. Soak up, for example, light rays
5. Colored material that absorbs some colors but reflects others
7. Color that results from mixing red and yellow pigments
8. Primary light colors are this type.
9. Primary pigments are this type.
13. Allows some light to pass without your being able to see through clearly
14. Type of nerve cells on retina that allow you to see dim light
17. Transparent object that allows one or more colors through but absorbs others
18. What an object does to light so we see it

Down

1. Light produced by mixing all colors of the visible spectrum
2. Colors that can be mixed to produce any other colors
4. Color of an object that absorbs all light
6. Nerve cells you use to distinguish colors
10. This type of radiation lies just outside the high-frequency end of the visible spectrum.
11. Allowing nearly all light to pass through
12. What you see when reflected wavelengths of light reach your eyes
15. Material you cannot see through
16. The color you see if you are looking at light that has no red or blue

---

Chapter 19
REINFORCEMENT

● Battle of the Bulbs

1. Write a paragraph about lighting. Use the words listed below in your paragraph.

light bulb   tungsten   phosphorus   light
incandescent light   heat   coating   efficiency
fluorescent light   filament   ultraviolet radiation

Accept all reasonable paragraphs.

_____

_____

_____

_____

_____

_____

2. Observe incandescent and fluorescent lights in your home, in your school, and in a store or office.

a. Where is each type of light more likely to be used? **Fluorescent lights are more likely to**
be used in stores and offices. Incandescent lights are used more extensively in

homes.

b. Compare and contrast the color and general appearance of fluorescent and incandescent
lights. **In general, incandescent lights give a more pleasant and warmer color of light**
than do fluorescent lights. However, some fluorescent lights have special colors and
are more like incandescent lights. Depending on the size of the bulb, both types of
bulbs can give out plenty of light.

c. Why do you think the types of lights were chosen for use in the places that you observed?
For home use, the color of the incandescent bulb is softer and has a warmer feel.
Also, most home lamps are designed for incandescent bulbs. For business use,
fluorescent lights are cooler and use far less energy. When a large number of fixtures
are in use, the cost of lighting a facility becomes a major consideration.

Chapter 19

REINFORCEMENT

● Wave Properties of Light

Fill in the blanks in this diagram of a light wave hitting a smooth, shiny surface.

FIGURE 1

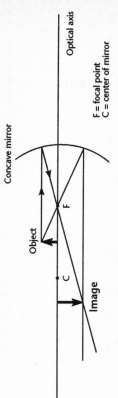
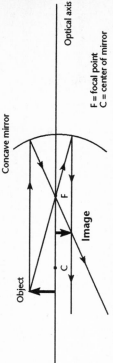

normal

angle of incidence

angle of reflection

incident wave

reflected wave

Figure 2 is a sketch of Tanya's fish tank as she looks at it from one of the corners. It appears to Tanya that there are two fish in the tank. However, she knows she has only one fish. Explain why two fish are seen and draw a ray diagram to show what happens. (Hint: The aquarium glass refracts light rays.)

FIGURE 2

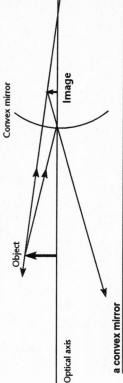

F_1 F F_2

a   b

Light rays a and b from the fish, F, are refracted producing two images that appear to come from F_1 and F_2.

On the blank, write the letter of the term that best completes each of the following statements.

c   1. The interference of light shows the _____ behavior of light.
　　a. particle　　b. translucent　　c. wave　　d. refraction

b   2. The bending of light around corners is called _____ .
　　a. refraction　　b. diffraction　　c. interference　　d. reflection

a   3. A(n) _____ is used to separate the colors of white light.
　　a. diffraction grating　　c. photon
　　b. electromagnetic spectrum　　d. modulation

Chapter 20

REINFORCEMENT

● The Optics of Mirrors

1. Locate the image of an object placed between the focal point and the center of a concave mirror by drawing two rays. Draw the image and describe this image with words.

Concave mirror

Object

C

F

Image

Optical axis

F = focal point
C = center of mirror

The image of the object is real, enlarged, and upside down.

2. Locate the image of an object placed beyond the center of a concave mirror by drawing two rays. Draw the image and describe this image with words.

Concave mirror

Object

C

F

Image

Optical axis

F = focal point
C = center of mirror

The image of the object is real, inverted, and smaller than the object.

3. What type of mirror would you use to allow a large area to be viewed?   **a convex mirror**
Use rays to show how a virtual image is formed by a convex mirror.

Convex mirror

Object

Image

Optical axis

a convex mirror

Why do you often see the phrase "Objects are closer than they appear!" written on convex mirrors?

Because the images of objects appear smaller than the actual objects, it seems that the objects must be farther away than they are.

Chapter 20

REINFORCEMENT

The Optics of Lenses

In the blank at the left, write the term that correctly completes each statement.

concave   1. A type of lens used to correct nearsighted vision is a(n) _____ lens.

refract   2. All lenses have a special property. This property is the ability to _____ light.

convex   3. A magnifying glass is an example of a(n) _____ lens.

retina   4. With normal vision, the image of an object should focus on the part of the eye called the _____.

astigmatism   5. The problem of blurry vision from _____ results from an uneven surface of the cornea.

6. Nearsighted vision is the result of the images of objects being focused in front of the retina.

Draw the type of lens in front of the eye below that would be used to correct nearsighted vision. Draw a ray diagram to show how this type of lens corrects nearsighted vision.

Chapter 20

REINFORCEMENT

Optical Instruments

1. You are going to assemble a refracting telescope, a reflecting telescope, and a microscope. Which lenses or mirrors will you put in each instrument? Write your answer in the table, using the lenses or mirrors from the list below. Each can be used more than once if needed.

concave mirror
convex lens
plane mirror

Refracting telescope	Reflecting telescope	Microscope
convex lens	concave mirror	convex lens
convex lens	plane mirror	convex lens
	convex lens	

2. Label the parts of this camera using the following terms: aperture, film, lens, and shutter.

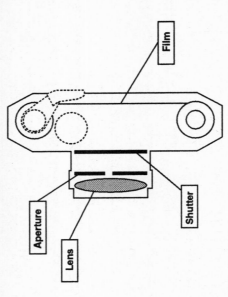

Complete the following paragraph.

Cameras use one or more lenses to focus light on photographic _____ **film** _____.

To focus the light, refraction by the lens creates a _____ **real** _____ image. The light

reaches the film only when the _____ **shutter** _____ is open. The shutter must be kept

open longer when the light is _____ **dim** _____. Another control of the amount of

light to reach the film is the _____ **aperture** _____ setting. Cameras can have removable

lenses so that lenses of different _____ **focal** _____ lengths can be used.

Chapter 20

REINFORCEMENT • The Hubble Space Telescope

Use with Text Pages 572–573

Write a paragraph describing the Hubble Space Telescope. Use the following terms in your paragraph.

distortion	primary mirror
images	secondary mirror
orbit	computer software
infrared	investigation
ultraviolet	

Hubble	
galaxies	
universe	
expanding	
solar panels	

Accept all reasonable paragraphs.

_____
_____
_____
_____
_____
_____

Describe the problems and setbacks faced in launching the Hubble Space Telescope into orbit. Use the following terms in your description.

late	software	redesign	delay	testing

Accept all reasonable paragraphs.

_____
_____
_____
_____
_____
_____
_____
_____

Chapter 20

REINFORCEMENT • Applications of Light

Use with Text Pages 574–579

Use two or three sentences to respond to the following questions.

1. Why are sunglasses with polarized lenses often worn by people driving long distances? **Light reflected from a horizontal surface, such as a highway, is partially polarized horizontally and is called glare. Polarizing sunglasses are made with vertically polarizing filters to block out most of the glare while allowing vertically polarized light to pass through.**

2. What is laser light? **Laser light is a beam of coherent photons, which are photons traveling in the same phase and in the same direction.**

3. Laser light has many practical uses. Briefly describe its use in the following areas.

a. retail stores and grocery stores **Lasers are used to read bar codes.**

_____

b. home entertainment systems **Lasers are used to play discs in your compact disc player.**

c. medicine **Lasers are used to cut through body tissues, to reduce bleeding by sealing off blood vessels, and for eye surgery including cataract removal.**

d. industry **Lasers can be used to cut and weld materials.**

e. surveying **Lasers can be used to measure great distances.**

f. astronomy **Lasers have been used to measure the moon's orbit, and also to measure the distance from Earth to the moon.**

g. communications **Lasers provide a coherent light source for fiber-optic communications.**

4. What are optical fibers? What are some of their major uses? **Optical fibers are transparent glass fibers that can pipe light from one place to another. Optical fibers are used in communications where one optical fiber can carry thousands of phone conversations at the same time. In medicine, physicians can use fibers to examine body parts that would otherwise be very difficult to reach and examine visually.**

NAME   DATE   CLASS

Chapter 20
REINFORCEMENT

● Electric Charge

Use with Text Pages 592–597

Determine whether the italicized term makes each statement true or false. If the statement is true, write the word "true" in the blank. If the statement is false, write the term that makes the statement true.

true	1.	The positively charged particles in an atom are *protons*.
electrons	2.	The negatively charged particles of an atom are *neutrons*.
true	3.	If an atom has an equal number of protons and electrons, the entire atom is electrically *neutral*.
negative	4.	If an atom has a greater number of electrons than protons, the entire atom has a *positive* charge.
static electricity	5.	The accumulation of electric charges on an object is called *magnetism*.
strongest	6.	The electric field caused by an electron is *weakest* near the electron.
true	7.	An electric field becomes weaker as distance from the electron *increases*.
true	8.	A conductor is a material that allows electrons to flow through it *easily*.
good	9.	Metals are *poor* conductors of electricity.
insulators	10.	Plastics, rubber, wood, and glass are good *conductors*.
true	11.	Earth serves as a *conductor* of electricity.
true	12.	The presence of electric charges can be detected with an *electroscope*.
no charge	13.	The leaves of an electroscope hang straight down when the device receives a *charge*.
repel	14.	If both leaves of an electroscope receive a negative charge, the leaves will *attract* each other.
positive	15.	When an object loses electrons, it gains a *negative* charge.

Copyright © Glencoe/McGraw-Hill, a division of The McGraw-Hill Companies, Inc.

87

NAME   DATE   CLASS

Chapter 21
REINFORCEMENT

● To Burn or Not

Use with Text Pages 598–599

Put the following illustrations showing the formation of lightning in the proper order by writing the numbers 1 (first) through 3 (last) in the spaces provided.

FIGURE A

FIGURE B

FIGURE C

___3___ A

___1___ B

___2___ C

In the spaces provided, explain what is happening in Figures A, B, and C above.

Figure A: As the difference in the negative charges in the cloud and the positive charges on Earth increases, electrons in the form of lightning are transferred from the cloud to Earth.

Figure B: Charged particles in a cloud become separated to form areas of positive charges and areas of negative charges within the cloud.

Figure C: As the bottom portion of the cloud gains a negative charge, it induces a positive charge at Earth's surface.

Answer the following questions on the lines provided.

1. How can lightning-induced forest fires be helpful to the environment? Fires burn away dead undergrowth while sparing mature trees, thereby preventing more serious fires.

2. Why do many buildings have lightning rods? Lightning rods channel electricity from the structure of the building and into the ground, preventing fire and injury.

88

Copyright © Glencoe/McGraw-Hill, a division of The McGraw-Hill Companies, Inc.

150

Chapter 21

REINFORCEMENT

• Electric Current

Circle the term in parentheses that makes each statement true.

1. A negatively charged object has electrons with (more, lesa) potential energy to move and do work than an object that is neutral.

2. Electrons flow from areas of (higher, lower) potential energy to areas of (higher, lower) potential energy.

3. Potential difference is measured in (amperes, volts).

4. Electrons passing through a lamp (gain, lose) some potential energy as they light the lamp.

5. Electrical potential (varies, is the same) in all parts of a circuit.

6. The current in a circuit is measured in (volts, amperes).

7. Current is measured with (an ammeter, a voltmeter).

8. When a dry cell is connected in a series, the flow of electrons moves from the (positive, negative) terminal to the (positive, negative) terminal.

9. In a dry cell, the carbon rod releases electrons and becomes the (positive, negative) terminal.

10. The potential difference between the two holes in a wall socket is (12 volts, 120 volts).

11. A car battery is an example of a (dry, wet) cell.

12. Resistance is measured in (ohms, volts).

13. Copper has a (higher, lower) resistance to electron flow than aluminum.

14. According to Ohm's law, ($I = V/R$, $V = I/R$).

15. The symbol for ohm is (Ω, π).

16. In the equation $I = V/R$, I is expressed in (ohms, amperes).

17. In the equation $I = V/R$, V is expressed in (volts, ohms).

18. The (+, –) terminal of a dry cell identifies the location of the carbon rod.

19. A wire with a resistance of 3Ω has a (greater, lesser) resistance to electron flow than a wire with a resistance of 5Ω.

20. A coulomb is the charge carried by 6.24 (billion, billion billion) electrons.

Chapter 21

REINFORCEMENT

• Electrical Circuits

Use the diagrams to answer the following questions.

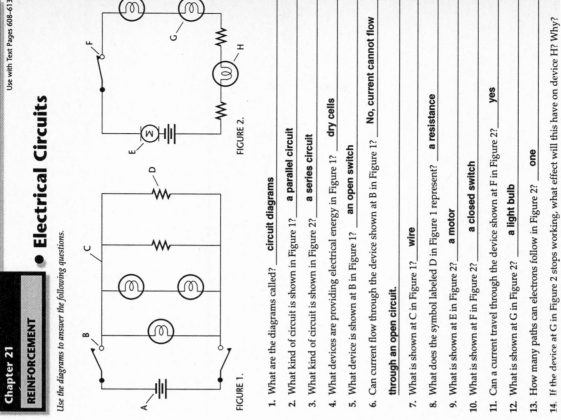

FIGURE 1.

FIGURE 2.

1. What are the diagrams called? __circuit diagrams__

2. What kind of circuit is shown in Figure 1? __a parallel circuit__

3. What kind of circuit is shown in Figure 2? __a series circuit__

4. What devices are providing electrical energy in Figure 1? __dry cells__

5. What device is shown at B in Figure 1? __an open switch__

6. Can current flow through the device shown at B in Figure 1? __No, current cannot flow through an open circuit.__

7. What is shown at C in Figure 1? __wire__

8. What does the symbol labeled D in Figure 1 represent? __a resistance__

9. What is shown at E in Figure 2? __a motor__

10. What is shown at F in Figure 2? __a closed switch__

11. Can a current travel through the device shown at F in Figure 2? __yes__

12. What is shown at G in Figure 2? __a light bulb__

13. How many paths can electrons follow in Figure 2? __one__

14. If the device at G in Figure 2 stops working, what effect will this have on device H? Why? __The device at H will also stop working because electrons will be unable to flow to this device since this is a series circuit.__

Chapter 21
REINFORCEMENT

● Electrical Power and Energy

Match each unit in Column II with what it measures in Column I. Write the letter of the correct unit in the blank on the left.

Column I	Column II
c 1. potential difference	a. W or kW
e 2. current	b. Ω
a 3. electric power	c. V
d 4. electrical energy	d. kWh
b 5. resistance	e. A

Use the equation P = I × V to find the missing value in each problem. Be sure to use the correct units in your answers.

6. A radio operates with a potential difference of 9 volts. The radio uses 0.9 watt of power. How much current does the radio use?

$P = I \times V$ $0.9\ W = I \times 9\ V$ $I = \dfrac{0.9\ W}{9\ V} = 0.1\ A$

7. A blow dryer uses 1200 watts of power. Current flow through the blow dryer is 10 amperes. At what potential difference does the blow dryer operate?

$P = I \times V$ $1200\ W = 10\ A \times V$ $V = \dfrac{1200\ W}{10\ A} = 120\ V$

8. A lamp operates with a potential difference of 120 volts and a current of 0.25 ampere. How much power does the lamp use?

$P = I \times V = 0.25\ A \times 120\ V = 30\ W$

9. A lamp uses 60 watts of power. It operates with a potential difference of 120 volts. How much current is required by the lamp?

$P = I \times V$ $60\ W = I \times 120\ V$ $I = \dfrac{60\ W}{120\ V} = 0.50\ A$

Use the electric meter readings in the table to answer the following questions.

Month	Reading (kWh)
June	6921
July	7923
August	9484

10. How many kilowatt-hours of electricity were used in the 1-month period between June and July?

7923 kWh − 6921 kWh = 1002 kWh

11. How many kilowatt-hours of electricity were used in the 1-month period between July and August?

9484 kWh − 7923 kWh = 1561 kWh

12. If electricity costs $0.16 per kilowatt-hour, how much would the electric bills be for the periods June–July and July–August?

June–July period: 1002 kWh × $0.16/kWh = $160.32
July–August period: 1561 kWh × $0.16/kWh = $249.76

Chapter 22
REINFORCEMENT

● Characteristics of Magnets

Complete the diagrams below as instructed or answer the questions.

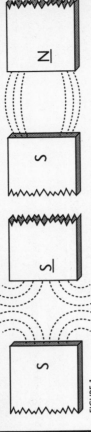

FIGURE 1.

1. The lines in Figure 1 show magnetic forces acting between two pairs of bar magnets. Correctly label the unlabeled poles of the magnets. Write **N** for north and **S** for south on the proper part of each magnet.

2. What generalization can you make about the reaction between like poles?

Like poles repel each other.

3. What generalization can you make about the reaction between unlike poles?

Unlike poles attract each other.

4. On Figure 2, draw the lines of force around the bar magnet as they would appear if you sprinkled iron filings around the magnet.

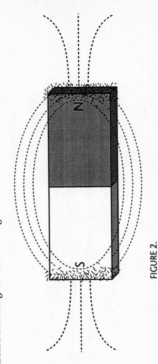

FIGURE 2.

5. Where are most of the iron filings located? __at the poles__

6. Where are the iron filings most spread out? __at the center of the magnet__

7. What can you infer about the strength of a magnetic field based upon the position of the iron filings? __**The magnetic field is strongest at the poles of a magnet and weakest near the center of the magnet.**__

8. What three materials can be used to make a magnet such as the ones shown above?

__iron, cobalt, and nickel__

Chapter 22
REINFORCEMENT

Use with Text Pages 628–632

● Uses of Magnetic Fields

Circle the term in parentheses that makes each statement true.

1. When a current is passed through a coil of wire, (an electromagnet) a commutator) is formed.

2. An electromagnet is a (permanent, (temporary)) magnet.

3. Adding more turns to the wire coil ((increases) decreases) the strength of an electromagnet.

4. Increasing the amount of current that flows through a wire ((increases) decreases) the strength of an electromagnet.

5. Electromagnets change electrical energy into (chemical, (mechanical)) energy.

6. An instrument that is used to detect current is (an electromagnet, (a galvanometer)).

7. Ammeters are used to measure the (potential difference, (electrical current)) passing through a circuit.

8. The potential difference of a circuit is measured in (amperes, (volts)).

9. The potential difference of a circuit is measured with ((a voltmeter) an ammeter).

10. An ammeter should be connected ((in series) in parallel) with a circuit.

11. A reversing switch in a motor that rotates with an electromagnet is called a (voltmeter, (commutator)).

12. Billions of nuclei in your body respond to an applied magnetic field when you have (an X ray, (an MRI)).

The table below compares and contrasts the characteristics of ammeters and voltmeters. Complete the table by filling in the information requested.

Characteristic	Ammeter	Voltmeter
What it measures	electric current	potential difference
How it's connected	in series	in parallel
Units of measurement	amperes	volts

Chapter 22
REINFORCEMENT

Use with Text Pages 633–639

● Producing Electric Current

Study the diagram below. In the spaces provided, label each drawing as either a motor or a generator. Label parts a–h as either coil, brushes, commutator, permanent magnet, or shaft.

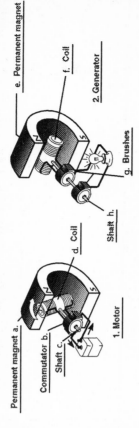

Permanent magnet a. _____

Commutator b. _____

Shaft c. _____

d. Coil

1. Motor

e. Permanent magnet

f. Coil

g. Brushes

Shaft h. _____

2. Generator

Circle the term in parentheses that makes each statement true.

1. When the wire loop of a (motor, (generator)) turns, an electric current is produced.

2. The current produced by a generator is (direct, (alternating)) current.

3. A motor ((uses) creates) an electric current as it turns.

4. A device that increases or decreases voltage of a power line is a ((transformer), motor).

5. If the secondary coil of a transformer has more turns than the primary coil, the transformer is a ((step-up) step-down) transformer.

In the space below, draw a sketch of a step-down transformer that has half as many coils in the secondary coil as it has in its primary coil.

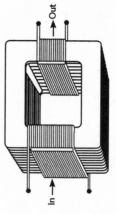

In ↓   Out ↑

Student sketches will resemble this one.

Chapter 22
REINFORCEMENT

Use with Text Pages 640-641

• Superconductivity

Determine whether the italicized term makes each statement true or false. If the statement is true, write the word "true" in the blank. If the statement is false, write in the blank the term that makes the statement true.

__increases__   1. As the temperature of a material increases, its resistance *decreases*.

__true__   2. Materials that have no electrical resistance are called *superconductors*.

__0 K__   3. Absolute zero is *zero degrees Celsius*.

__critical__   4. The temperature at which a material becomes a superconductor is called its *resistance* temperature.

__true__   5. Because superconductors have no resistance, a current can flow through them *indefinitely* without losing energy.

__heat__   6. Ten percent of the electrical energy that flows through power lines is lost as *light*.

__brittle__   7. It is hard to shape superconducting materials into wire because they are *flexible*.

__true__   8. Levitating trains do not give off *pollutants*.

__true__   9. A material that allows electrons to flow through it easily is a *conductor*.

__helium__   10. One way to cool a material to its superconducting temperature is to immerse it in liquid *copper*.

__true__   11. New materials have been developed that are superconducting at temperatures as high as *120 K*.

__true__   12. Resistance in a material causes energy to be lost as *heat*.

Chapter 23
REINFORCEMENT

Use with Text Pages 648-653

• Semiconductor Devices

Determine whether the italicized term makes each statement true or false. If the statement is true, write the word "true" in the blank. If the statement is false, write in the blank the term that makes the statement true.

__semiconductors__   1. Materials that are less conductive than metals but more conductive than nonmetal insulators are *magnets*.

__true__   2. Some *metalloids* are semiconductors.

__true__   3. The conductivity of semiconductors can be *increased* by adding impurities to semiconductor crystals.

__true__   4. The ability of *transistors* to amplify signals makes it possible to use tape recorders and television.

__metalloids__   5. In the periodic table, all the elements located between the metals and nonmetals are *semiconductors*.

__rectifier__   6. A device that can change alternating current to direct current is a *transistor*.

__true__   7. A diode allows *current* to flow in only one direction.

__semiconductors__   8. Today's radios can be extremely small because they have *magnetic electrical tape* instead of vacuum tubes.

__true__   9. A semiconductor that increases the strength of an electrical signal is a *rectifier*.

__amplification__   10. The process by which the strength of an electric current is increased is called *transition*.

__true__   11. An integrated circuit contains resistors, transistors, and diodes on a thin slice of *silicon*.

__less__   12. Electronic equipment that uses integrated circuits requires *more* space than equipment that uses vacuum tubes.

__increases__   13. Doping silicon with arsenic *decreases* its conductivity.

__rectifier__   14. The adapter for a radio is a type of *integrated circuit*.

Chapter 23

REINFORCEMENT ● **Radio and Television**

Use with Text Pages 654–657

Use the diagram below to answer questions 1–5.

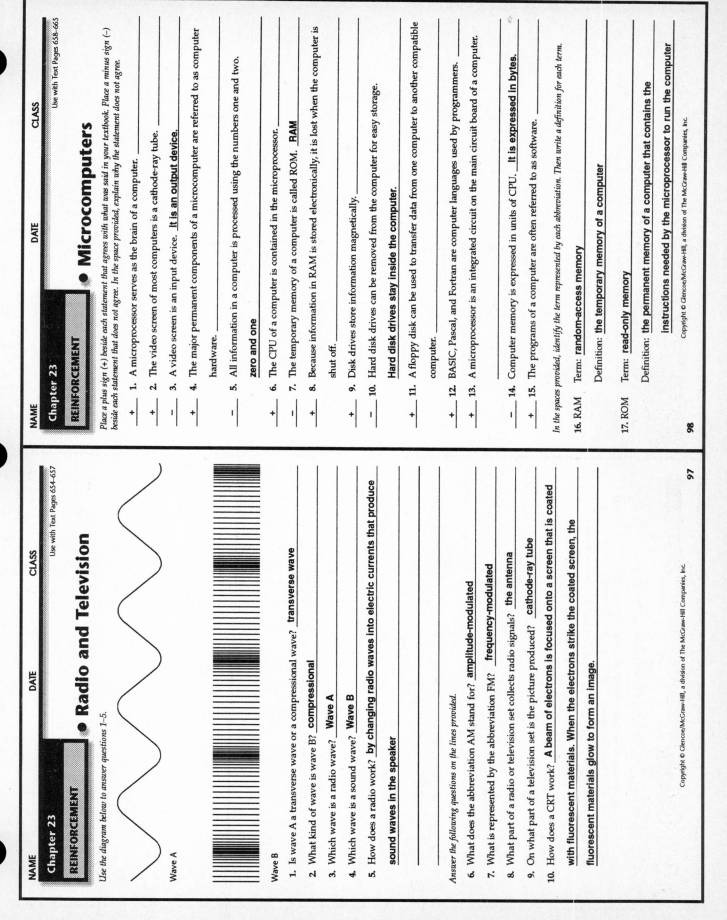

Wave A

Wave B

1. Is wave A a transverse wave or a compressional wave? __transverse wave__

2. What kind of wave is wave B? __compressional__

3. Which wave is a radio wave? __Wave A__

4. Which wave is a sound wave? __Wave B__

5. How does a radio work? __by changing radio waves into electric currents that produce__ __sound waves in the speaker__

Answer the following questions on the lines provided.

6. What does the abbreviation AM stand for? __amplitude-modulated__

7. What is represented by the abbreviation FM? __frequency-modulated__

8. What part of a radio or television set collects radio signals? __the antenna__

9. On what part of a television set is the picture produced? __cathode-ray tube__

10. How does a CRT work? __A beam of electrons is focused onto a screen that is coated__ __with fluorescent materials. When the electrons strike the coated screen, the__ __fluorescent materials glow to form an image.__

Chapter 23

REINFORCEMENT ● **Microcomputers**

Use with Text Pages 658–665

Place a plus sign (+) beside each statement that agrees with what was said in your textbook. Place a minus sign (–) beside each statement that does not agree. In the space provided, explain why the statement does not agree.

+ 1. A microprocessor serves as the brain of a computer.

+ 2. The video screen of most computers is a cathode-ray tube.

– 3. A video screen is an input device. __It is an output device.__

+ 4. The major permanent components of a microcomputer are referred to as computer hardware.

– 5. All information in a computer is processed using the numbers one and two. __zero and one__

+ 6. The CPU of a computer is contained in the microprocessor.

– 7. The temporary memory of a computer is called ROM. __RAM__

+ 8. Because information in RAM is stored electronically, it is lost when the computer is shut off.

+ 9. Disk drives store information magnetically.

– 10. Hard disk drives can be removed from the computer for easy storage. __Hard disk drives stay inside the computer.__

+ 11. A floppy disk can be used to transfer data from one computer to another compatible computer.

+ 12. BASIC, Pascal, and Fortran are computer languages used by programmers.

+ 13. A microprocessor is an integrated circuit on the main circuit board of a computer.

– 14. Computer memory is expressed in units of CPU. __It is expressed in bytes.__

+ 15. The programs of a computer are often referred to as software.

In the spaces provided, identify the term represented by each abbreviation. Then write a definition for each term.

16. RAM   Term: __random-access memory__

Definition: __the temporary memory of a computer__

17. ROM   Term: __read-only memory__

Definition: __the permanent memory of a computer that contains the__ __instructions needed by the microprocessor to run the computer__

Chapter 24

REINFORCEMENT ● **Radioactivity**

Use with Text Pages 674–678

Use the following section of the periodic table to complete the following.

55 Cs	56 Ba	71 Lu	72 Hf	73 Ta	74 W	75 Re	76 Os	77 Ir	78 Pt	79 Au	80 Hg	81 Tl	82 Pb	83 Bi	84 Po	85 At	86 Rn
87 Fr	88 Ra	103 Lr	104 Unq	105 Unp	106 Unh	107 Uns	108 Uno	109 Une									

57 La	58 Ce	59 Pr	60 Nd	61 Pm	62 Sm	63 Eu	64 Gd	65 Tb	66 Dy	67 Ho	68 Er	69 Tm	70 Yb
89 Ac	90 Th	91 Pa	92 U	93 Np	94 Pu	95 Am	96 Cm	97 Bk	98 Cf	99 Es	100 Fm	101 Md	102 No

1. Use a pencil to lightly shade in the boxes of the radioactive elements.
Students should shade the boxes containing elements 83–109.

2. Draw an X through the boxes that represent synthetic elements.
Students should draw an X in boxes 93–109.

3. How many of the radioactive elements are found in nature? ____10____

4. How many radioactive elements are made only in the laboratory? ____17____

5. What statement can you make about the relationship between atomic numbers and
radioactivity? ____**All elements with an atomic number of 83 or higher are radioactive.**____

The atomic mass of uranium is 92. The most stable isotope of uranium is uranium-238. The radioactive isotope of uranium is uranium-235. In the spaces provided, write the symbols for the nuclides of each isotope of uranium. Then, answer the questions.

Uranium-238	Uranium-235
$^{238}_{92}U$	$^{235}_{92}U$

6. How many neutrons does uranium-238 contain? ____146____

7. How many neutrons does uranium-235 contain? ____143____

Chapter 23

REINFORCEMENT ● **Computer Crimes**

Use with Text Pages 666–667

Decide whether each action described below is a computer crime. Write "Y" in the blank if it is a computer crime. Write "N" in the blank if it is not a computer crime.

N 1. You make a backup copy of software you purchased to use if the original becomes damaged.

Y 2. You make a copy of software you bought to give to a friend.

Y 3. A friend of yours gives you a copy of the software needed to play a computer game.

N 4. You discover that a disk you borrowed from a friend has placed a virus in your computer.

Y 5. You decide to play a practical joke on someone by placing a computer virus into his computer system.

N 6. You can access the library computer from your computer. When you input the information needed to get into the subject files, you discover that you have actually accessed the overdue books file.

Y 7. You use a password you have discovered to get into the school's computer system and change your grade in algebra.

N 8. You and your friend are working together on a project for school. You both have the same program in your computers and decide to exchange discs once a week to transfer information from one computer to the other.

Answer the following questions on the lines provided.

9. How does a computer virus interfere with a computer? __It uses up memory and may__ __cause a computer to stop functioning.__

10. How can you help to protect your computer system from an attack by a virus? __Use an__ __antivirus program.__

11. Why is hacking an invasion of privacy? __Hacking involves breaking into the private__ __documents of individuals or companies without permission. These__ __documents are intended to be seen only by authorized people; therefore__ __access to these documents by unauthorized persons is an invasion of__ __privacy.__

Use with Text Pages 679–685

● Nuclear Decay

Element Z has a half-life of one week. Use the graph grid and the directions below to trace the decay of a 256-gram sample of element Z over a 10-week period. Each box on the grid represents one gram of element Z. After you complete each step, answer the question.

Week

Directions and Questions

1. Use a pencil to draw a large X through all of the boxes on the left half of the grid. How many grams of element Z decayed? **128 g**

2. Use a different color pencil to draw a large X through 1/2 of the remaining boxes. How many grams of element Z remain after two weeks? **64 g**

3. Use your pencil to shade 1/2 of the remaining boxes. How many grams of element Z are left? **32 g**

4. Repeat step 3 using the colored pencil. How many grams of element Z remain? **16 g**

5. Use a pencil to draw an X in 1/2 of the remaining boxes. How many grams of element Z remain? **8 g**

6. Repeat step 5 using the colored pencil. How many grams of element Z remain? **4 g**

7. Use your pencil to draw a circle in 1/2 of the remaining boxes. How many grams of element Z remain? **2 g**

8. Repeat step 7 using the colored pencil. How many grams of element Z remain? **1 g**

9. Shade in 1/2 of the remaining box with your pencil. How much of element Z remains? **0.5 g**

10. Repeat step 9 using the colored pencil. How much of element Z remains? **0.25 g**

On a separate sheet of graph paper, make a line graph or a bar graph that shows the decay of element Z over a 10-week period. Use your answers to questions 1–10 as your data.

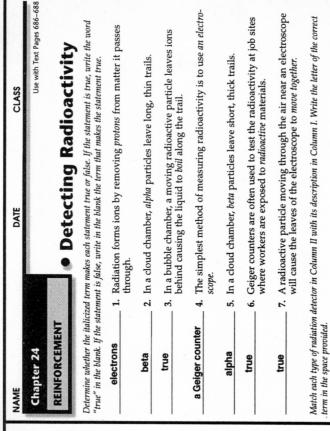

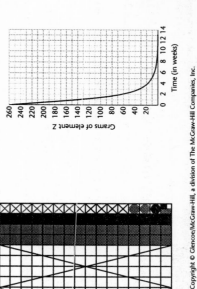

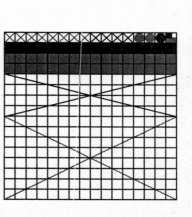

Use with Text Pages 686–688

● Detecting Radioactivity

Determine whether the italicized term makes each statement true or false. If the statement is true, write the word "true" in the blank. If the statement is false, write in the blank the term that makes the statement true.

__electrons__ 1. Radiation forms ions by removing *protons* from matter it passes through.

__beta__ 2. In a cloud chamber, *alpha* particles leave long, thin trails.

__true__ 3. In a bubble chamber, a moving radioactive particle leaves ions behind causing the liquid to *boil* along the trail.

__a Geiger counter__ 4. The simplest method of measuring radioactivity is to use *an electroscope*.

__alpha__ 5. In a cloud chamber, *beta* particles leave short, thick trails.

__true__ 6. Geiger counters are often used to test the radioactivity at job sites where workers are exposed to *radioactive* materials.

__true__ 7. A radioactive particle moving through the air near an electroscope will cause the leaves of the electroscope to *move together*.

Match each type of radiation detector in Column II with its description in Column I. Write the letter of the correct term in the space provided.

Column I	Column II
__c__ 8. Ionizing rays pass through a superheated liquid.	a. Geiger counter
__d__ 9. Ionizing rays pass through a supersaturated vapor.	b. electroscope
__b__ 10. loses charge in the presence of radiation	c. bubble chamber
__a__ 11. Radiation causes current to flow from a wire to produce a clicking sound or flashing light.	d. cloud chamber

• Using Nuclear Reactions in Medicine

Use with Text Pages 692–695

On the lines provided, identify the radioisotope that would most likely be used to diagnose or treat a problem for the organ shown.

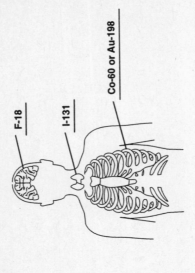

F-18

I-131

Co-60 or Au-198

Answer the following questions on the lines provided.

1. The most stable form of iodine is iodine-126 with an atomic number of 53. How many neutrons does an atom of I-126 contain? __73__

2. How does iodine-131 differ from iodine-126? __Iodine-131 has 5 more neutrons than Iodine-126__

3. Cobalt usually has an atomic number of 27 and an atomic mass of 59. How does an atom of Co-60 differ from an atom of Co-59? __Co-60 has an additional neutron.__

4. A stable technetium (Tc) atom has an atomic mass of 98 and an atomic number of 43. How many neutrons does an atom of technetium-99 have? __56__

5. How many protons does Tc-99 have? __43__

In the spaces provided below, write the symbols for the nuclides of the most common isotopes of iodine, cobalt, and gold. Then write the symbols for the nuclides of the radioisotopes of each element.

	Iodine	Cobalt	Gold
Common Isotopes	$^{126}_{53}\text{I}$	$^{59}_{27}\text{Co}$	$^{197}_{79}\text{Au}$
Radioisotopes	$^{131}_{53}\text{I}$	$^{60}_{27}\text{Co}$	$^{198}_{79}\text{Au}$

• Nuclear Reactions

Use with Text Pages 689–691

Use the diagram below to complete the following activities.

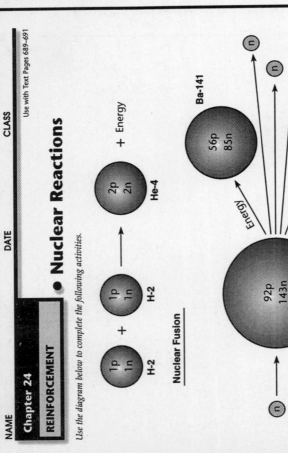

1p 1n   +   1p 1n   →   2p 2n   + Energy
H-2   H-2   He-4

Nuclear Fusion

92p 143n
U-235

Energy

Energy

56p 85n
Ba-141

36p 56n
Kr-92

n   n   n

Nuclear Fission

1. The diagram shows two types of nuclear reactions: nuclear fission and nuclear fusion. Label the type of reaction shown in each diagram in the space provided.

2. Circle the letter of the equation that correctly explains the nuclear reaction shown in the top diagram.
   a. H-2 + H-2 → H-4   (b.) H-2 + H-2 → He-4   c. H-1 + H-1 → H-2   d. H-1 + H-1 → He-2

3. Circle the letter of the equation that correctly explains the nuclear reaction shown in the bottom diagram.
   (a.) 1 neutron + U-235 → Ba-141 + Kr-92 + 3 neutrons
   b. 1 neutron + U-238 → Ba-141 + Kr-92 + 4 neutrons
   c. Ba-141 + Kr-92 → U-235 + 3 neutrons
   d. Ba-141 + Kr-92 → U-238

4. What two elements are involved in the nuclear fusion reaction? __hydrogen and helium__

5. Label each atom in the fusion reaction with its correct symbol and isotope notation.

6. What three elements are involved in the fission reaction shown? __uranium, krypton, and barium__

7. Label each atom in the nuclear fission reaction with its chemical symbol and its correct isotope notation.

Use with Text Pages 700–703

Chapter 25
REINFORCEMENT

Fossil Fuels

Complete the table below by placing a check mark (√) beneath the headings of the substances that have each characteristic described in the first column.

Characteristic	Petroleum	Natural Gas	Coal
1. Is a fossil fuel	√	√	√
2. forms from plants and animals	√	√	
3. forms only from plants			√
4. Is a solid			√
5. Is a liquid	√		
6. Is a gas		√	
7. is made up of hydrocarbons	√	√	√
8. Is a source of energy	√	√	√
9. is a nonrenewable resource	√	√	√
10. is pumped from wells	√	√	
11. is separated using fractional distillation	√		
12. is also called crude oil	√		
13. is transported long distances through pipes	√	√	
14. is mined from Earth			√
15. produces polluting substances when burned	√	√	√
16. produces thermal energy when burned	√	√	√
17. can be used to produce electricity	√	√	√
18. is the least polluting fossil fuel		√	

Use with Text Pages 704–709

Chapter 25
REINFORCEMENT

Nuclear Energy

Place the following events describing the production of electrical energy from a nuclear fission reactor in the correct order. Write the numbers 1 (first) through 7 (last) in the spaces provided.

5   a. Steam produced by boiling water causes the blades of a turbine to rotate.

1   b. A neutron bombards a uranium-235 isotope.

3   c. Thermal energy released by the reaction is added to water.

7   d. Electricity from the generator is carried to the community through wires.

2   e. A uranium-235 atom splits, producing two atoms with smaller nuclei, three neutrons, and thermal energy.

6   f. The mechanical energy of the rotating turbine blades is transferred to an electric generator.

4   g. Superheated water passes through a heat exchanger, where the thermal energy released boils a separate system of water to produce steam.

Answer the following questions about nuclear energy.

1. How does using nuclear energy harm the environment? **Uranium must be mined from Earth. The mining of uranium causes environmental damage.**

2. How is using nuclear energy less harmful to the environment than using fossil fuels? **Unlike the burning of fossil fuels, the use of radioactive substances to produce electricity does not cause air pollution.**

3. How does the half-life of a radioactive waste affect the type of container in which the waste will be stored? **Radioactive wastes may have very long half-lives. If a waste is to be stored in a container, the container must be made in such a way that it will last the duration of the period of radioactive decay.**

4. Why is nuclear fusion not currently used as an energy source on Earth? **The temperature required to carry out a nuclear fusion reaction is too high for the reaction to be carried out in a laboratory.**

5. How do the products of a fusion reaction differ from the products of a fission reaction? **The products of a fusion reaction are not radioactive. The products of a fission reaction are radioactive.**

Chapter 25

REINFORCEMENT • Nuclear Waste and NIMBY

Circle the term or phrase in the parentheses that makes each statement true.

1. At present, proposals are being investigated to store high-level nuclear wastes in containers placed in (dried-up river beds, (underground rock deposits)).

2. The spent fuel from a nuclear reactor must be stored because it is (low-level, (high-level)) nuclear waste.

3. At present, military nuclear wastes are stored in (a single location, (several locations)) in the United States.

4. One reason spent fuel rods must be disposed of in durable containers is that they contain material with (very short, (very long)) half-lives.

5. Low-level nuclear wastes from medical processes are usually disposed of by being ((buried in special landfills), burned).

6. Nuclear wastes are ((radioactive by-products), unused nuclear materials) that remain after radioactive materials are used.

7. At present, a national storage site for high-level nuclear wastes has been seriously proposed near (Oak Ridge, Tennessee; (Yucca Mountain, Nevada)).

8. One recent proposal involved in disposing of nuclear wastes is to ((seal them in ceramic glass globules), mix them with salt deposits).

9. The point of view that nuclear wastes should be stored but not in their immediate area is known as (NWPA, (NIMBY)).

10. If no new radioactive wastes were generated from today on, the problem of storage would (be eliminated, (still remain)).

11. One reason the federal government wants to establish a national, permanent storage site is that ((some temporary sites have shown leakage), transportation problems would be reduced).

In the space provided, answer the following questions about a single, national, underground storage site.

Answers will vary. All logical responses should be accepted.

12. What questions need to be answered before selecting a site? **What is the geology of the site? Will it be safe from underground shifts due to fault lines, or can it survive an earthquake of any severity? Would salt corrode the containers? Would it be better to have several scattered sites so radioactive wastes would not have to be transported long distances to a single site?**

13. What are the main points in favor of such a site? **Research shows that deep, stable rock deposits offer best hope for storing radioactive wastes safely. Strict federal design rules and safety standards could be maintained. Temporary sites have shown leakage. The Federal government is charged with establishing a national, permanent site by 2010.**

Chapter 25

REINFORCEMENT • Alternative Energy Sources

Provide the information requested for each alternative energy source listed.

1. Biomasses
   a. What is biomass? **renewable organic materials**
   b. How is biomass used? **It is burned to convert stored chemical energy to thermal energy.**

2. Solar energy
   a. What is solar energy? **energy from the sun**
   b. What is passive solar heating? **the direct use of the sun's energy in maintaining indoor temperatures**
   c. What is a photovoltaic cell? **a device that converts solar energy into electricity**

3. Hydroelectricity
   a. What is hydroelectricity? **electrical energy produced from the kinetic energy of moving water**
   b. What is one economic advantage to hydroelectricity? **Once a dam is built to harness the water, the cost of electricity is relatively cheap.**

4. Tidal energy
   a. What is tidal energy? **energy generated by the tidal motion of the oceans**
   b. Why is tidal energy a limited source of energy? **Only a few places have enough difference between high and low tide to be able to use this as a source of energy.**

5. Wind energy
   a. What device is used to harness the energy in wind and convert it into electricity? **a windmill**
   b. Why is the wind an energy source with limited uses? **Only a few areas have a consistent wind that can be relied on to generate electricity.**

6. Geothermal energy
   a. What is geothermal energy? **thermal energy in molten rock that lies far below Earth's surface**
   b. Where is geothermal energy used as a primary energy source? **Iceland**